WEST COUNTRY WITCHCRAFT

West Country Witchcraft

By

Gillian Macdonald and Jessica Penberth

GREEN
MAGIC

Green Magic
Long Barn
Sutton Mallet
Somerset TA7 9AR
England

Typeset by Academic and Technical, Bristol
Website: www.acadtech.co.uk
Printed by Antony Rowe, Chippenham

Cover production by Chloe Hayes
Cover design by Peter Gotto
Editing by James Capel

ISBN 978-0-9552908-2-4

GREEN MAGIC

Contents

Acknowledgements   vii

Greetings   ix

1 Witchcraft Past and Present   1

2 West Country Witches, Pellers and Charmers of Old   25

3 Modern Witchcraft in the West Country   51

4 Sites   81

*Dedicated to all those poor unfortunate souls who lost
their lives through being accused of witchcraft, may your
deaths not be in vain.*

Acknowledgements

From Gillian

Great thanks to Pete Gotto at Green Magic Publishing for all his help and patience whilst waiting for this book to arrive. Special thanks to Graham King and all at the Museum of Witchcraft in Boscastle for allowing me access to the library. Thanks also to my mum and all other family and friends too numerous to mention, especially Jessica Penberth for coming on board and co-writing this little book with me. And special thanks to the spirits of nature for keeping me sane in an insane world!

From Jessica

I would like to thank Gill for giving me the opportunity of joining her on this venture; it has been an exciting experience for me.

Also I would like to thank my husband David for all his love, support and encouragement for my new direction in life, without him I would still be stuck behind a desk going slightly mad. Respect also goes to Eddie who has helped me to be more confident within myself so that I can walk my path with my head held high.

Blessings

Gillian Macdonald (formerly Mary Neasham) and Jessica Penberth

Greetings

Wherever you find yourself travelling in the West Country you are bound to encounter evidence of Witchcraft, whether past or present.

Although divided into three counties, each with their own essence or unique energy, the whole of the West Country has been a safe haven for both the ancient Celts of our past and their magical beliefs and home to many a Witch although as we will see many of those Witches certainly wouldn't call themselves as such.

Witchcraft seems to be such a multi-levelled label with so many positive and negative connotations that it isn't that easy to accurately define, either as a personal archetype or magical practice.

It wasn't until the establishment of Christianity, especially Catholicism, on our shores that those who dabbled in sympathetic magic, spiritual healing, astrology and other mystical crafts were suddenly thought to be inspired by the Middle Eastern Devil and his legions of demonic beings all eager to grab your soul. Previously our Pagan European religious and cultural past hadn't conceived such a notion and the confusion that must have emerged from the new views being placed on our old Gods and Goddesses (who were each seen as dualistic: light and dark. Or in other words creative and destructive to a separation of two beings, one ultimately Good the other all Evil) can't have made much sense. Surprisingly, however, it worked. Why? Because in the new religious order that followed if you lead a good and wholesome life you were guaranteed a place in an afterlife, called heaven, when you died. That was suddenly everyone's goal.

For the magical minorities of the time it was a hard blow but many survived to hand their knowledge down. Such people had a name for their craft, though it was rarely used. They were practising the ancient art of *wicce*, Anglo Saxon for shaman, and so in time, *wicce* became witch.

This identifiable title set a precedent. Suddenly magic of any sort was evil as were any practitioners of these arts.

The old Celtic God Cernunnos and the Roman God, Pan were adopted as Devilish beings by the early Church, probably because of their wilder aspects. They were accused of luring people into evil ways, so both the physical appearance and psychological aspects of this Christian Devil were entrenched into the human psyche, where it has been ever since.

During this transitory period of spiritual change, fear of Demonic possessions, Witchcraft, sorcery, and anything that wasn't viewed by holy men of the time as ethically, morally, politically or socially palatable, was blighted and pursued as they saw fit.

This essentially middle eastern paranoia took a strong hold and by medieval times the then Catholic Church of Rome wrote The Hammer of the Witches, the infamous *Malleus Maleficarum* it set out to define witches and in particular, what they viewed as Witchcraft. This was essentially aimed at further suppression and disempowerment of women and was mostly geared towards them.

By Tudor times we were beginning to experience the sweeping tail of the European inquisition and although Reginald Scott wrote his entirely sensible book *The Discoverie of Witchcraft*, few took him seriously. Scott set out to discredit the fear mongers and murderers from taking hold of our shores and spreading their poison throughout our land. He painstakingly attempted to prove that Witches, as the Church viewed them, did not actually exist. In spite of his study they still burnt and hanged hundreds, if not thousands of innocent people all the same.

In reading a quote from the book, which refers to the treatment of women during the inquisition, one can see how strongly he felt about it;

> *And because it may appear unto the world what treacherous and faithless dealing, what extreme and intolerable tyranny, what gross and fond absurdities, what unnatural and uncivil discourtesy, what cankered and spiteful malice, what outrageous and barbarous cruelty . . . what abominable and devilish inventions and what flat and plain knavery is practised against these old women, I will set down the whole order of the Inquisition to the everlasting, inexcusable and apparent shame of all Witch mongers.*

I think we can safely say he put it well. In our eyes it was an overtly female act of genocide and one that all branches of the Christian Church to their discredit, still sweep under the carpet to this day. Yet, ironically, Christ was also accused of acts of witchcraft such as walking on water.

Later on in our British history James I a staunch Calvinist supporter and self proclaimed enemy of Witches, wrote the counter attack *Daemonologie*. Again inspiring fear, paranoia and hatred of anyone practising any form of magic amongst the people of the time. Many of these acts thought magical at the time, were often not as such. Gradually over time with the widening of scientific knowledge and continued acceptance of many magical country ways, they were eventually relegated on the most part to harmless folklore.

By the eighteenth century many had succumbed to our scientific and industrial revolution. With this came a widening acceptance and interest in the occult world, inspired partly by exposure to countries such as Egypt and its mysteries. The Hermetic Order of the Golden Dawn was founded in Glastonbury and many modern off-shoots of this Western magical mystery school are still evident today especially in the West Country.

Another example of tolerated folklore that endures to this day partly owes its origins to the terrible potato famines of Ireland.

Many new Irish migrants came to our shores during the eighteenth century bringing with them a resurgence of Celtic influences this added a new dimension to the fairy world with their leprechauns or Piskies and this re-enforced belief in the little folk a concept that already had a stronghold in the West of the country.

Due to its environmental limitations and continuity of customs and traditions, it doesn't surprise me to find that the West Country, by and large, escaped the more virulent attacks on magical people. Although some cases of Witchcraft were charged, heard and tried, there were very few compared to the East of the country.

The one overwhelming impression you get from visiting the West Country is that this place itself is magical. The *genius loci* or local spirits are tangible. You can sense them, Whether you are standing at the base of Glastonbury Tor looking up in awe or delving deep into Wookey Hole caves, or out wandering amongst the many stone circles and long barrows on our moors, each place has a strong spiritual resonance that you can actually perceive.

As you travel further west into Devon you can sense a slowing down of pace as though the spirits of each place are encouraging you to stop and take notice of them. The rolling, green, lush, ambrosia hills give a sense of safety and protection with their attractive little thatched villages and cosy corners. The open moor land of Exmoor gives a sense of space and majesty with its heath, craggy rock outcrops and surprisingly steep, hidden valleys. Here one can find peace and solitude amongst the heather and gorse of the brackland with wild Exmoor ponies, sheep and deer dotted about.

Coastal Devon is dotted with secret coves and dramatic cliff tops alive with nature and stunning views and is bestrewn with magical places to discover.

Then there is the incredibly dramatic and moody Dartmoor with its grey foreboding hills and bleakness interspersed with miles of grassland. Bogs, wait to catch unsuspecting travellers, are places of many a mystical tale and legends of ghosts. These superstitions still affect us to this day (though I will say though that its not a place to venture deep into without a stout pair of walking boots and a reliable compass).

Moving further west the scenes change yet again, each becoming slightly wilder than the last and rawer in its magical intensity. It's easy to understand how this place has become such a stronghold of myth and legend over time.

The north coast of Cornwall is mainly high slate and granite cliffs and coves that once were secret ports to many a smuggler. One such natural harbour, at Boscastle, is home to the infamous Witchcraft Museum. Bodmin Moor traverses part of central Cornwall. It is a bleak and haunted place of howling mythical hounds and megalithic stone circles not to mention the original Jamaica Inn (of Daphne De Murier fame).

Southern Cornwall is more relaxed, it's similar to areas such as the South of France, which is why most of the south west coast is affectionately called the English Riviera. It is the Western most parts of Cornwall, however, that have the most prolific Witchcraft connections and with place names such as Wicca Pool or the Witches stone at Zennor, one can see why. This area feels ancient, as if almost untouched by human hands it has an amazing energy that can really surprise you with its intensity and is most healing and inspiring.

The one overwhelming factor that always makes me feel completely at home every time I visit the West Country, is the people with their tolerance, acceptance and embrace of the world as a magical place. Here you can sense the respect for this craft or nameless art, a respect that one feels goes back a long way past our Christian heritage way back to our Pagan ancestors and even further still to our pre-historic shamanic roots.

It is this respect, understanding, knowledge and common sense that I feel draws many witches to the area each year. That and the wonderfully special, magically charged, sacred landscape we are all so lucky to belong to, that attracts all of us.

The misty dawns inspire an air of mystery. The vibrant mid-day sun illuminates the sacred landscape in a myriad of colours.

The setting sun of dusk over the ocean top cliffs weaves a spell of enchantment to any who take the time and trouble to just sit quietly and absorb the magic of these special places in the west.

So without prejudice I urge you to view the magical practitioners past and present with an open mind and thoroughly enjoy your own special, magical relationship with the West of our Country and its Witches!

1

Witchcraft Past and Present

It is almost impossible to discover the exact roots of what we now acknowledge as Witchcraft. The earliest Witches certainly hadn't ever heard of the label 'Witch' nor would they have considered their practises necessarily evil. They simply had 'their ways', strange mysterious ones at times, but each one responding to their own *wyrd* or self. Their knowledge could cover quite a wide spectrum. From healing with herbs or spells to incantations, mid-wifery skills and charms for lovers. Or from aiding a local farmer to rid his cows of disease, to stirring up a storm to bring ships to their perilous ends on the rocks near the shore. There are cases in which they attempted the opposite by aiding ships with a good wind. Many of them were most likely hereditary in their practice and each one seemed to have been afforded a particular magical gift.

Some appeared prophetic, some magical healers, some could read the stars or were early astrologers. It's interesting to note that astrology and astronomy were once combined sciences with astronomy becoming the more acceptable face of our later scientific revolution.

The very word Witchcraft conjures up both positive and negative associations. If you look at it from a neutral standpoint witchcraft seems to be about the use of magic and spells. One could say that 'magic' in its purest form is the art of changing consciousness and physical reality according to will. Human beings have used magic and spells since pre-historic times to enhance their daily lives and assert some control over the environment in which they live. The earliest evidence of magic dates from cave paintings of the Palaeothic Age, some of which suggest magic rituals were performed to secure a successful hunt. It is now thought that these paintings were often interpretations of dream images and deliberate trances but they are undoubtedly mans earliest attempts to record something of his imagination for prosperity.

Numerous definitions of magic have been offered by many who have practised and studied it. Yet magic eludes a precise description, it remains a very individualistic experience. Although every person who practises magic has their own take on it, many witches past and present tend to view it as a way of using your will to change things around you for the better, for yourself and others.

People often talk about white magic and black magic; to us magic doesn't have a colour, although we must say there is no light without shadow. Magic is neutral and amoral, as is nature; it is the intent of the practitioner that makes it good or bad, leaving personal responsibility for the consequences on the shoulders of the magician.

Modern Witchcraft contains elements of folk magic and ceremonial magic. A lot of folk magic was derived from the West Country. In the past the belief that you could magically influence some control over your environment was perhaps far more relevant than today. The West Country was once very cut off from the rest of southern England. Living conditions were incredibly tough with people at the mercy of the elements. With far less infrastructure to fall back on in hard times than we have today, winters were indeed very harsh times for all living in isolated rural areas, so they frequently turned to witches for help. By using magic and spells they could help to cure illness, ensure a good harvest and protect livestock. To do this the West Country Witch utilised whatever she or he had in the way of tools around them, hence items such as the broomstick and the cauldron becoming associated with Witchcraft. Herbs were commonly used along with other plants. As were stones found on the door step, especially those with natural holes which were thought to have magical properties.

Put simply a spell is a spoken or written formula that in a magical ritual is intended to cause or influence a particular course of events. Spells are closely related to prayer, which is a ritual consisting of a petition to a deity (or deities) for a desired outcome. Prayer involves visualisation of the goal, statement of desire for the goal and ritualised movements or body positions as in clasping of hands, kneeling etc. Spells are also closely related to various methods of mind power such as 'creative visualisation' or 'positive thinking'. All of which emphasise mental images, identification with those images, a clear goal, repetition of ones intent to achieve this goal, projection of will and invocation of the aid of spirits, deities or the divine force.

Spells can be beneficial or harmful and they may be worked on people, animals and nature in general. The purposes are endless and can include healing, love, money, success, fertility, longevity, protection, exorcism of ghosts, and limited localised weather control, amongst other things. As Witches were thought to be born not made the magical energy required to manifest their spells was inherent to them and unlike many of today's practitioners they didn't have to utilise any particular energy raising technique to reach their goals.

Although many of today's practicing witches don't like to be reminded of their ancestor's readiness to occasionally practice negative or destructive magic they never the less did so at times and there certainly is plenty of evidence to support this. When a negative spell is directed at an enemy it may cause sickness, destruction, loss of love, poverty, impotence, barrenness, failure and even death. One may cast a spell on oneself or one may direct it at another person. A positive spell is therefore considered as a blessing and a negative one as a curse. The more commonly used archaic terms for spells include bewitchment and enchantment. Negative spells are generally described as hexes or curses. A binding spell is however a difficult one to interpret and in our view definitely falls into a magical 'grey area'. On the one hand it can be seen as performed with the intent to prevent harm or disaster or to simply stop someone from performing a particular act (e.g. stopping a criminal or preventing gossip) and on the other hand it can be performed to literally bind someone to someone or something else and until broken will remain bound (e.g. binding lovers together).

In the West Country most villages had a cunning woman or man, someone who possessed psychic and healing powers and provided cures, remedies, charms, spells and divination, usually in exchange for a fee or small gift. They studied, noted and could predict natural effects such as weather changes, moon phases, and the movement of tides amongst other things. The term 'cunning' comes from the old English word '*keening*' or '*ken*' meaning to see or know a word still used to this day in Scotland. These would be the people that village folk could turn to for medicine, midwifery skills, and even aiding the passing over of the dying. They were there to assist in the whole cycle of life.

Traditionally cunning folk came into their craft by hereditary means but others acquired their gifts by supernatural intervention (e.g. fairies, the spirits of the dead or divine visions). The majority of the magic they performed prior to the Christian conversion was sympathetic magic but this gradually became an amalgamation of Christian prayers and rites mixed with pagan material. Folk magical arts were often passed on in an oral tradition, embellished and enhanced as time went on. The cunning folk were often described as odd people with strange or unusual appearances. Although it is now thought that much of the archive of visual images and engravings of the archetype witch show the poor woman as she appeared after being tortured by inquisitors. They were often easy prey as many lived alone or in semi-seclusion often choosing the company of their animals over other people.

Some witches charged fees or an acceptable barter for magical services, the monies exchanged were generally small amounts as most clients themselves had little money to spare. Generally they practiced their magic as an open secret conducting their business quietly so as to avoid prosecution. Many of the early recorded witches offered protection against evil from witch's bottles to amulets to complex invocations the local wise woman

Figure 1. Witches disturbed escape on broomsticks up the chimney.

or cunning man could provide any protection you required lest you fall prey to the evil eye. This evil eye is probably one of the most misunderstood concepts relating to the history of Witchcraft and it simply refers to anyone you think might have it in for you. It is entirely possible that many of the early Witches (and I use the term lightly) entered into a silent psychic war each one protecting those paying from other witches and even each other possibly creating a Witches mafia!

As mentioned in the introduction, the actual word 'Witch' seems to have originated from the Anglo-Saxon *wicce,* a term used to describe a shaman or medicine person. The origins of the word 'shaman' come from Siberia, so we can see how even thousands of years ago humanity was travelling about, sharing their knowledge and indeed their magic! The original *wicce* of the West Country would have practised both positive helpful magic and, if required, negative destructive magic also. Although some chose to tread a lighter path, not all did. Their decisions were probably based on the ethics they inherited with their craft, the morals of their time and their individual needs. This becomes more understandable if you happen to be old and fragile living on scraps in a remote area and are suffering from plain old fashioned hunger a concept we in the West are generally unfamiliar with today.

During the time of the Witch hunts many who were wrongly accused of Witchcraft were not Witches at all but just religious or political scapegoats or victims of the instability of their time. We suspect that any who did have genuine magical knowledge began to keep it to themselves or simply upped the ante on protection spells, inadvertently cashing in on the very fever that was heading their way. Or maybe it was simply a case of: '*Thank you so much for giving us the Devil to protect people from it will serve us quite well also, such a shame they made him out to appear like our favourite spring god though*' Many religious bodies have also profited extremely well from the Devil it must be said.

Historically the very acts of pagan worship that many of the cunning folk practiced were gradually labelled as Witchcraft. Though we doubt many mid-wives of today would think themselves Witches and for the most part it is still a name that is used as an insulting term.

As an example of the many and indeed varied historical recorded witchcraft accusations in the West Country we include this one from *The Western Morning News*.

'*At the Liskeard police court on Monday, Harriet King appeared before the sitting magistrates charged with an assault on Elizabeth Wellington. The complainant had called the mother of the defendant a witch and said she had ill-wished a person, the ill-wish had fell upon the cat and the cat had died. This annoyed the daughter, who had retaliated by bad words and blows. The magistrates expressed surprise at the cause of the assault, they fined the defendant 1 shilling and the costs came to £1 in all*'.

Ill-wishing is a curse that is the product of anger, envy and fear. Frequently in the past people blamed their misfortunes on the ill-wishing of others. If two people argued and then one suffered a mishap, became ill or had a set back the other party was suspected of ill-wishing them. Remarks such as 'you'll be sorry' were taken seriously as a form of negative Witchcraft. If somebody enjoyed a great deal of good fortune or prosperity and later suffered problems they believed themselves to be a victim of secret ill-wishing of envious friends or neighbours. The remedy for ill-wishing was to seek out the local Witch, peller or charmer and have the ill-wishing broken or neutralised with a charm. If the identity of the ill-wisher was not known, magic or divination was performed to expose them.

The peller is a healer, diviner and breaker of spells. The word itself originates from the Cornish '*pellhe*' meaning 'to cast away' and could also be linked with expel. As above the peller would be sought out if a person thought they were bewitched or cursed. Sometimes the mere mention of 'going to the peller' was sufficient for stolen goods to be returned or apologies made for any grievances. It was also customary to make annual visits to the peller just to have ones 'protection' renewed against bad luck and any acts of Witchcraft that might be directed ones way. This trip was done in spring as it was believed that the increasing of the Sun's energies at this time magnified the power of the peller. Despite the importance of the peller in the village few pellers lived solely upon their craft. Most were poor and held other jobs while they performed their magical services on the side.

Pellers were believed to acquire their gifts through hereditary or supernatural means. In Cornwall pellers were said to be descended from Matthew of Cury whose spell-breaking powers reputedly were bestowed upon him by a mermaid who he rescued and returned to the sea.

A famous peller who resided in the South west was said to be in possession of no end of charms and to posses powers of no common order over this and the other world. A friend wrote that 'he is able to put ghosts, hobgoblins and I believe even Satan himself to rest. I have known farmers, well informed in other matters, and members of religious bodies to go to the peller to have the spirits that possessed the calves driven out;

for they, the calves, were so wild they tore down all the wooden fences and gates and must be possessed by the devil'.

The peller always performed a cure but as the evil spirits must go somewhere the peller in this case made it imperative that a stone wall was built around the calves to confine them for three times for seven days, or until the next moon is as old as the present one. This precaution seemed to result in taming the devils and the calves. The peller then sent the spirits to some very remote region magically chaining them under granite rocks.

Another case of ill-wishing happened to an old woman who had suffered for a long time from debility; she thought she had been ill-wished, so she went to the peller. He told her to buy a bullocks heart and get a packet of pins. She was to stick the heart all over with pins, the body that ill-wished her felt every pin run into the bullock's heart the same as if it had been run into them. The spell was taken off and the old woman grew strong again. Another similar example tells of an old man living on Lady Downs who had a lot of money stolen from his house, he too went to the peller. In this case the magician performed the spell and the man was told his money would return. After a few days, during the night, the money was tied to the handle of the door and found there by the rightful owner the following morning.

Pellers made charms for their clients from herbs, powders, ointments, potions, stones and perhaps even teeth and bones were often used as was dirt from graveyards. These were placed in little bags to be worn around the neck as an amulet. A great deal of secrecy surrounds the art of the peller, clients were admonished not to talk about any of the proceedings between them and the peller. Pellers were active well into the 19th Century and a few can be found in rural areas to this day.

Charms have been used since ancient times. Some charms are verbal, a phrase, formula or prayer, whilst others are inscriptions on paper, parchment, wood or other materials even animal skin that can be worn on the body of the afflicted. Charms exist for virtually every desire and purpose; to secure or lose a lover, ensure chastity, fertility and potency, gain victory, riches and fame or exact revenge. Other charms protect crops and farm animals, milking and churning butter or rid one of rats, vermin and weeds. All of the above were so important to the people in the West Country who relied heavily on agriculture and livestock.

The pellers and cunning folk often used Christian prayers spoken or written in Latin, or debased Christian prayers. The Church approved the use of prayers and scriptures as cures and protection against evil but disapproved of the prescription of them by pellers and charmers.

One such example is the Witches bottle, a common charm used in folk magic to protect against evil spirits and magical attack, was also utilised to counteract spells cast by witches. Traditionally, the witches' bottle was a little flask about three inches high and made of blue or green glass. The witches' bottle was prepared magically by the peller or cunning folk who frequently put the victim's hair, nails or urine into it. When the bottle was buried beneath the house hearth or threshold the spell was nullified and the witch supposedly suffered great discomfort. Sometimes the bottles were thrown into the fire; when they exploded the spell was broken and the witch potentially killed. If urine was used as a counter-charm then the witch would retain urine and be unable to pass water and was thus exposed for her maliciousness that caused the harm to humans or animals. Witches bottles were also used to nullify the evil eye. They would be hung in chimneys as charms to protect the owners from witches flying down their chimneys at night and entering the house. They were also hung next to doors and windows and plastered into walls above lintels to protect the threshold. Commercial buildings, rail lines, bridges and other structures were often given witches bottles as protection against evil and or disaster.

Witches boxes were particularly popular in the 16th and 17th century and they usually consisted of a small wooden box with a glass front, filled with herbs, bits of rowan, pieces of human bone and odds and ends, over which a magic spell of protection has been cast. From the 18th century onwards witch balls became more fashionable and were often hung in windows to ward off witches and ill fortune. These were decorative glass balls that measured up to seven inches in diameter and again they were usually blue or green although some were silvery to act as convex mirrors. As they were similar to the glass balls used by Cornish fishermen they were associated with many sea super-stitions and legends.

Much of the magic used by the cunning folk was sympathetic magic; the connection of objects and events by association. Similar shapes, colours, smells or symptoms for example. The symptoms of the common cold such as swollen, red, running eyes and nasal discharge are duplicated when cutting an onion. So it is strongly held, even now, that onions were a cure for a cold. It is only recently that science has caught up and found that both onion and garlic have anti-bacterial properties. There was, and often is, a link or connection between items used for the ailment or ill-ness and what was around them in nature. Dock leaves are most commonly thought to be a cure for nettle stings because the two grow together and therefore cure and disease must be associated. But it has been said that it's the sap of the nettle stalk that is the antidote and the dock leaves were supposed to be used to grasp the nettle whilst you broke the stem to extract the sap to rub on the sting although it appears that some of this knowledge has been lost over time.

Ringworm was rife on many farms and spreads like wild fire so it was common practice to call in the local cunning folk to help charm the ringworm. The most common objects to have been used as ringworm charms were circular, like the mark left by the ringworm so gold rings were often used as sympathetic magic to make the ringworm go away. In reality ringworm is a fungus that once exposed to sunlight often recedes in a few weeks but in winter months, when animals were crowded into damp cold barns, ringworm would thrive.

Wart charming was also a common occupation for the cun-ning folk. A lot of the old spells that were used involved positive visualisation of the wart getting smaller. In fact there are wart charmers still around today who only have to think about the wart disappearing for it to shrivel up and magically disappear. We know this to be true after a successful charm to rid Gill's dog of a nasty eye wart.

Another popular method was to cut a potato in half and rub the cut side onto the wart before putting the two halves of the potato together again and burying them in the ground, as the potato rots so does the wart. Similar methods involve rubbing the wart with bean pods or bacon rind, as above in each case the pods and rind must be buried immediately after application. As they decay so will the warts, the results being based on sympathetic magic. The outcomes are completely satisfactory, implying that the actual methods employed have little or no bearing on the subsequent cure.

A curious fact about wart charming is the variety of methods used by charmers. There is no standard cure nor are herbal remedies normally used. Each practitioner acts in accordance with their own individual ideas, whims or hereditary custom. One of the most common is simply the shaking of hands with the charmer. Another is for the charmer to buy the patients warts. In some cases the coin must be carefully preserved or else the warts could return. In others the coin must be discarded instantly, a classic example of the often contradictory nature of magic.

A Dartmoor woman described how, when she was young she was taken to have her warts cured by an old lady who lived at Holne. She was required to pay three visits, taking with her a blackthorn, wool from a white sheep and milk from a red cow. The witch kept the thorn and the wool but the milk was preferred fresh every time, possibly a useful addition to the larder. The witch held the thorn, dipped the wool in the milk and anointed the warts, which then disappeared.

Counting plays a part in several of the methods used. Some witches will instruct the patient to go home, count his or her warts and put the equivalent number of small stones or pebbles into a bag which they must then throw away, preferably at a crossroads. The danger of picking up any package found lying by the wayside was a well known superstition so it was unlikely to be disturbed. If, however, curiosity overcame caution the packet or parcel should be kicked first to ascertain its contents for should it contain 'wart stones' the finder could automatically transfer the warts to themselves.

A young farm hand described how he had several ring worms on his hand caught from the cattle he was tending. The village witch looked at his hands and asked how many patches he had. The lad gave the number and was told he would have no further trouble with them. Nor did he, but when he got undressed that night he discovered several new patches on his back that he'd been unaware of. In a few days time those on his hands had cleared up but the ones on his back persisted. Now it's entirely possible that the ones on his hands were exposed to the sunlight and those on his back were still in the dark, ringworms favoured environment.

Bean pods also figure in another curious incident that was relayed by a country parson. A reputed witch had died in his parish and during the time in which her body lay in the kitchen-living room of her cottage odd physical manifestations occurred, which he himself witnessed. Showers of bean-pods kept falling down the chimney on to the empty hearth. Investigations of both chimney and roof were made, but everything appeared normal. The pods continued to fall at regular intervals until the funeral after which they ceased as mysteriously as they had started.

Another example of sympathetic magic is an old Dartmoor remedy for chilblains. To get rid of them all that are needed is to wish them onto a recently deceased person. Here the sympathetic link is between the coldness of the dead body and the chill that caused the blain; although as anyone who has suffered from them knows the irony is they cause an intense burning sensation.

A sloughed viper skin was often used to aid the extraction of thorns which is another example of sympathetic magic with the thorn being akin to the bite of the viper. A snakes skin is drawn off at the appropriate season, as the reptile rubs its length along the bushes, therefore, it was reasoned the discarded skin would draw out the thorns and splinters. This seems to be a fairly straight forward chain of thought, but oddly enough the skin was to be applied to the part of the hand opposite the thorn, which would then be repelled into a natural withdrawal.

Snake lore is a fascinating and exhaustive subject, the harmless grass-snake and the venomous adder can both be found in the bogs and heather of Dartmoor and Bodmin. These areas are rich in charm lore against many things but especially the adder. Both reptiles were treated with extraordinary fear and dislike by the average countryman and were often battered to death, neither is as common now as it was even a few years ago and the snake population is decreasing annually. Up until recently it was commonly believed that the only recovery from an adder bite was to ensure the death of the offending snake. Until this was accomplished the patient, it is thought, would not recover. When cattle or dogs fall victims to bites from the adder it is rarely seen. In this case, when the animal began to show improvement from the bite it was conveniently assumed that the reptile met its death 'somehow else'.

One moor man called John once sought help from a Belstone witch. Leaving his dog, which was to all appearances dying from a snake bite at home. *'Have you killed the adder?'* was the only question the woman whose help he procured, asked. Receiving an affirmative reply she merely said *'very well go home and you'll find your dog alright'*. He did and was met by the door by his tail wagging spaniel which he'd left for dead in an apparent coma.

A curious superstition attached to a reptiles death is that 'a snake can't die 'till the sun goes down'. It's battered corpse may be left flattened on the road, but according to local lore, it cannot be considered officially or safely dead until sunset. Another old superstition is that where a viper lies concealed a dragon fly hovers above, sent by providence to give warning of danger. This is sometimes heard of as the Dartmoor guardian angel!

Two old country remedies were recommended for the adders bite. Should a dog fall victim out in the wilds beyond the reach of a witch or a vet, a hazel wand, if obtainable should be twisted into a ring and placed around the animal's neck, representing a magic circle of protection. The second remedy is plainly a herbal 'simple'. Upon reaching home, fresh green ash-tips should be gathered and boiled, the resulting liquid being given to the dog as medicine. Both of these remedies were commonly used in the West Country until relatively recently.

Local cunning folk were often visited with people who had been bitten by adders whereupon they would apply a toad skin to the bite as toads were believed to be immune from snake bite, probably on account of the thick leathery texture of their skins. To accompany this act of sympathetic magic, repelling poison by something itself considered poison repellent, there was an old charm or blessing:

Adder, Adder, Adder, lay under a stone or hole he hath done this beast wrong. I fold, two, fold three, fold in the name of the father and of the son. So let this sting pass away from this wretched vermint, if the Lord pleases, Amen.

The cunning folk were very 'in tune' with nature and their surroundings and it was this that they often turned to for help with spells and charms. One such slightly unorthodox example of this can be found at the Museum of Witchcraft in Boscastle. A woman who wanted to stop her man from straying too far from home took one of his 'stools', yes we did say that, and put it into one of her stockings then placed it into the attic of their home. This ingenious use of objects found round and about the home seemed to stop her husband from getting up to no good and having affairs and serves as a reminder to many men about the resourcefulness of their loved ones! Though why she used the 'turd in a stocking' instead of something potentially less smelly and offensive is anyone's guess.

Witches also relied on magically charged equipment utilising that which was readily to hand, with the broomstick and cauldron being two of the most well known items. There are various hypotheses as to why the broomstick is associated with witches. One is that brooms are a symbol of female domesticity, a tool of everyday women and as most witches are women they would use their most common tool and soar up the chimney with it! Another is the link relating to pagan fertility rites to induce pregnancy and or crops to grow. People mounted brooms, poles and even pitchforks riding them like hobby horses in the fields, dancing and leaping high into the air. This ancient festival is still practised in the West Country with the most popular and well known 'Obby Oss' day held in Padstow on 1st May.

As we have seen the witches 'craft' is constantly evolving with each witch differing slightly from each other in all aspects. But it must be remembered that the 'craft' of the witch is deeply woven into nature and its cycles. So ingrained into the folklore, religion, local environment and even our politics that it is both inseparable and yet indefinable at the same time.

There are many myths relating to Witches some of which have grains of truth in them yet others have been somewhat exaggerated or twisted to suit. Let us look at the most popular ones:

Consorting with the Devil

The cloven-footed horny chap we are all familiar with seems to have evolved from both the Celtic/Germanic Horned God of the woodlands, Cernunnos and the Greek God Pan. These Gods were representative of spring and male fertility and did indeed have overtly sexual festivals; this sexy image was borrowed for the early Catholic Christian personification mainly due to their belief that sex was only important for reproduction. Enjoying sex was therefore seen as sinful and only tolerated within marriage.

Thankfully this view has changed and most people have their own personal morals and ethics relating to it these days. There are many who still view it as sacred and indeed either the highest form of magic, or more simply part of the divine gift of love and life.

Burning in Hell

This relates to the underworld or the resting place of the dead but owes its origins to the Norse and Anglo-Saxon goddess Hel who was the guardian of the dead and offered new life or re-birth through her springs or well waters. The irony of this myth is that the original underworld was thought of as frozen not a burning hell. This makes perfect sense if you think of the places that Hel originated from were pretty icy in the winter, making you were more likely to die from hypothermia than burn for your sins in places such as Scandinavia.

Hooked noses, pointy hats and broomsticks

So do modern witches have hooked noses?

A few might, not that it matters.

Do they wear pointy hats?

Figure 2. The horned God.

Only when attending fancy dress parties in my experience but cloaks with hoods were once pretty common attire and often appear pointed. There is also evidence of large copper wizard style hats or crowns having been found on the continent which might have been worn during magical rituals.

Do they ride broomsticks?

Yes and no. The traditional besom broom was used almost exclusively by most people, up until just over one hundred years ago as the most common form of domestic broom. It is now used by people who call themselves witches as both a practical broom and a magical tool for casting protective magical circles or sweeping out negative energy from the house. As for flying, well only astrally but not literally.

Do witches use cauldrons?

Some still do. The cauldron or cooking pot was once the main receptacle that everyone used for boiling and cooking in until relatively recently in historical terms. It is believed that the notion of the witch's cauldron originates from the Welsh goddess Cerridwen who was thought to have a magical cauldron of infinite knowledge that she scryed in. Many modern witches do own cauldrons and use them for both scrying and mixing 'potions' and yes frogs legs and eye of newt do come into it but only in so much as they are West country nick names for particular plants and herbs (much as Dragons Blood has nothing what so ever to do with mythical beasts but is in fact a form of incense).

There is, however, a tradition of Toad witches in the East of England and this might be where the myth originated from and one can see how these misunderstandings and deliberate perversions may have occurred.

Witches Familiars

Familiars were thought to be demons in animal form that were used for the purpose of carrying out spells and bewitchments.

Figure 3. Seventeenth-century woodcut of witches.

The most common were in the form of cats, toads, owls, mice and dogs although virtually any animal or insect could be suspected of being such. Familiars (also called imps) were said by God-fearing Christian folk in medieval times to be given to the witch by the Devil or bought or inherited from other witches. A witch could have several of them. Cats were thought to be favoured, especially black ones. The fear that cats were witches familiars was one of the reasons for the cat massacres that swept through medieval Europe. Familiars were given names like any household pet. Familiars were believed to be dispatched to bewitch people and animals into sickness and death. They also protected the witch.

More benevolent familiars were believed to exist in the service of the cunning folk or pellers who were magicians and village healers. The familiars helped diagnose illnesses and the source of bewitchment often used for divining and finding lost items or treasures. They were conjured with rituals and then locked into bottles, rings or stones and sometimes sold as charms, in turn claiming the spirits would ensure success in gambling, love or business.

Many modern witches have animal familiars, usually cats, which are magical helpers although dogs, birds, snakes or toads are also popular. Modern witches don't believe their familiars are 'demons' or spirits in animal form but simply animals whose psychic attunement makes them ideal partners in magic. Familiars are reputedly sensitive to psychic vibrations and power and are welcome partners inside the magic circle for the raising of power, casting of spells, scrying, spirit contact and other magical work. They also serve as psychic radar, reacting visibly to the presence of any negative or evil energy, whether it is an unseen force or a physical presence. Familiars are also given psychic protection by their owners. Some witches also use the term familiar to describe thought forms created magically and empowered to carry out a certain task on the astral plane.

Familiars are also linked with the supposed shape shifting abilities of Witches. This area may well be one of the oldest and most intriguing of the Witches myths. This intimate, yet non-sexual relationship with animals probably goes right back to our more shamanic roots and a time when our everyday lives were more interdependent and far closer to animals and nature generally. The myth of shape shifting stems from the shamanic practise of taking on the spirits of animals by process of dance and trance, usually under the effect of some sort of hallucinogen, to establish possession of a particular beast especially in regards to hunting and medicine.

Mankind's relationship with the animal kingdom has shifted many times throughout our history. Once we hunted and gathered following herds of edible cloven beasts aided by the knowledge gained by watching wolves and the nature of all our cousins of the hunt. Settling and farming changed this, as did the later arrival and reading of the Bible that encouraged us to see the animal kingdom as ours to master and do with what we will, leading to a less respectful relationship with nature in general.

Some animals we became closer to than others and it is interesting to note that those we have such fondness for now were once as wild as lions are today.

Dogs were encouraged as they could help us with hunting. Cats were tolerated, even venerated in some cultures because they ate the vermin that lived off our gathered grain. Horses held pole position for thousands of years both as transport and food, this list could go on and on.

But the Witches cat was seen as special, as more than just a mouse catcher, and in many respects this was true. So many of the women accused of Witchcraft were solitary, lonely and poverty stricken. Their cat might have been their only company or comfort so it is unsurprising that they had a close relationship. Cats are mystical creatures in their own right in that they choose to be with us never having been entirely mastered or tamed by mankind. They are still regarded as wild animals in this country and it is extremely difficult to command any mastery over one. If a cat isn't happy where it is then it will simply move on. They are natural healers almost instinctively knowing when someone is in pain or ill and naturally migrating to that person to sit on their lap and purr, sending positive healing vibrations into the afflicted. Even the cat's purr is still a mystery that to this day science hasn't completely explained. It is agreed by most that it does appear to be a form of healing mechanism. A happy and appreciative cat will often hunt on our behalf, bringing in offerings of rabbits, pigeons, squirrels or rats for our pleasure. Although this isn't always appreciated I've yet to meet a totally selfless dog who does this out of instinct.

The cat, whether male or female, has always had a link with the feminine in humanity. It is seen as a promiscuous creature of the night, so we can see how Witches have been linked to such feline activity.

Cats are often good early warning signals and we have all come across the old wives tale that if a cat washes behind its ears then it might rain.

In my experience cats will often find people and not the other way around. Of course it is possible to buy a cat and even ensnare it in a house, but cats by their nature are semi-tameable and don't take kindly to becoming house cats. Most prefer their freedom and perhaps it is that which frightened the paranoid men of the persecution times most of all.

The notion of flies being Witches magical imps appears to be a fictitious invention by the Witchcraft persecutors, who also perpetrated the concept of 'The Devils Mark', increasing the fear of warts and birth marks as being signs of a Witch. But as for flies, the very idea is ridiculous.

Is Halloween the Witches' night?

No. All Hallows Eve is the night believed by both Christians and pagans to be a special night when the veil between the dead and the living is thin. It is celebrated as a night to remember and/or contact ones ancestors. The night is often referred to as Samhain which originates from the Celtic tradition.

Are gypsies the true witches?

This is a difficult area. There are some that believe many of the ancient mysteries and herbal lore came from wandering Gypsies or Romanies bringing their knowledge from the East. The travelling nomadic families would absorb a little from each culture they moved through, adding to their own language and knowledge as they went. This was an oral tradition as very few Romanies were literate. It's entirely possible that they introduced palm reading, reading tea leaves, crystal ball reading and Tarot cards into our country but only by virtue of the fact that these were practises they picked up and mastered as they travelled along. To the local indigenous person, who might not have ever travelled further than a few miles from home the Romany or gypsy 'ways' must have appeared magical and mysterious. They simply 'knew' more about people because they encountered more of them and built up a greater or bigger picture of humanity in all its diversity. The word 'hex' seems to have originated from the Germanic word Hexe, meaning to curse or wish ill. The gypsy curse is a powerful psychological tool, and I for one am not going to discredit its ability to work, having said that, there are many who call themselves Gypsy (or to be more accurate, Romany) who are not. Authentic

Figure 4. Gypsy Smith – Jeannette's Aunt.

Romanies are fairly rare in this country these days, most being Irish or Scottish travellers. There is a saying that a true Romany friend of mine agreed with when we said it to him; *Ki shani Romani, Adoi san I chou'han,* in other words, 'where Romany's go, so will witches be found'.

Are witches really Devil worshippers or Satanists?

There may well be some who claim to be Satanists and we cannot be sure who exactly they are getting in contact with by doing so. This is a difficult area for it seems those accused of Witchcraft in the past were believed to be so and the vast majority of those practising Witchcraft openly today denounce the very notion of a Devil. It is possible that those calling themselves Satanists today are simply exploring their own darkest corners and the reflection of such evil and cruelty in mankind as a whole.

We haven't as yet come across anyone in the West Country who openly admits to following this path but have decided it's very much a case these days of each to their own.

So do witches join covens and run around naked in the woods?

Yes, some do but only a very few. There is at least one form of Wicca or modern witchcraft that prefers to commune with their God and Goddess sky clad or naked. They believe it is a purer way of relating to divine spirit and greatly levelling, no doubt, but they are pretty rare. There were the odd reports of some covens in the sixties and seventies indulging in group ritual sex. This was probably more to do with the sexual revolution than any deeply held religious or magical beliefs. Of course it is completely possible that there are sexually interactive covens existing but we haven't, as yet, met any. Most people think it is actually too cold in this country for such al fresco behaviour. Witches covens or groups do exist and usually prefer to keep quiet about it, mainly due to prejudice. The few we know of are very good people who join up seasonally to give benign or personal offerings and say their thanks to the deities or spirits they believe in. They have no other hidden group agendas. Some groups are what we'd describe as 'open covens' that also hold seasonal rituals where everybody gets a chance to equally contribute.

We conclude that the vast majority of modern Witches don't believe in the Devil but just like all of us they do believe in wrong doings and harmful acts. They also appear to believe it is up to all of us to wrestle with our own consciences over what constitutes an act of 'evil' and take individual responsibility for ones self and ones actions.

Modern witchcraft or its interpretation thereof, is increasing in popularity today and appears at surface value to be a form of communion with the divine spirit through the elements of nature on a magical level. For many it is a personal path of spiritual growth, whereupon one aims to become a better person through states of heightened awareness of self. It is of course much more complicated than that so should you wish to investigate this further there are literally hundreds of books available on the subject for you to read.

So, yes here in the West Country and many other parts of the world there are witches.

Modern witches, yes, but owing their origins to the people who once hunted by the moon and planted by the sun. Who lived closer to the land and nature in general and understood its patterns and cycles. Who mastered magical crafts such as herb craft, divination, astrology, illusions or harmless trickery, spells and wishes, amongst many others. Who's amalgamated and titled conceptions of Witch is rooted in the persecuted masters and mistresses of the past and now proud to say, 'Yes, I'm a Witch'.

2

West Country Witches, Pellers and Charmers of Old

Have you ever heard tell of the wicked witch of the West, and if so did you think this was merely an imagined character or creative archetype? Well yes and no, there was a very well known and renowned Witch of the West but she wasn't considered an entirely wicked person as such.

Thomasine Blight alleged she was born in 1798 reputedly in the town of Redruth in Cornwall but even this is possibly a story perpetrated by the lady herself. The earliest parish records place her in Gwennap just south west of Redruth where her baptism occurred on 4th August, 1793.

For a woman of the early nineteenth century she married late in life to a bachelor named Richard Blight, a stone mason by trade. The wedding took place in the merry month of May in 1825 at St. Euny. She subsequently bore three children but only one survived, the other two succumbing to illness at a young age.

After a couple of house moves the couple eventually settled in Redruth in 1831 and it is presumed this was for practical reasons as Redruth was then a prosperous copper and tin mining valley. Sadly Richard, her husband, died in the summer of 1832 of typhus leaving Thomasine a widow with one son, Henry, to support and the potential of a bleak future in the workhouse looming over them. It is believed that Thomasine was already building her reputation as conjurer and wise woman whilst married to Richard

Figure 5. Thomasine Blight – The Witch of The West.

and that she acquired some basic education and literacy skills from him whilst they were together. Eventually she met James Thomas, a part time cunning man who also worked the mines. Although twenty one years her junior James took the widowed Thomasine as his wife and they married just before Christmas in 1835.

For the next fifteen years they built upon their joint reputations as magical divinators, spell casters and enjoyed a conjuring double act. Her working name was Tammy Blee and many came to her for cures for disease for themselves, their families and their livestock. They were able to build up considerable business by reputation and although they succeeded in this they eventually made another move, this time to Helston. Their main customers appeared to have been farmers seeking cures for their beasts and protection of crops. These regular protection spells became almost like insurance policies of the time with strange yet sympathetic methods employed by James and Tammy. One of Tammy's rather cabbalistic preferences was the power of magical squares, one of which was thought to have originated from Roman Pompeii as seen below.

R	O	T	A	S
O	P	E	R	A
T	E	N	E	T
A	R	E	P	O
S	A	T	O	R

Pieces of paper with these words written on them were often found in charm bags for protection.

It's important to remember that in these remote areas during the nineteenth century, where science and medicine was only in its infancy, people still believed in the power of ill wishing or black magic and often would accredit any illness or condition or lack of luck to one of these things. Wise men and women proficient in sympathetic, or white magic, could earn a reasonable living by offering to rid people of these afflictions or protect them by magical means.

One of Tammy's most infamous yet controversial jobs appeared when a labourer called upon her services to literally raise the spirit of his formerly wealthy yet deceased employer. As heir to her estate, he'd been unable to find either her will or any evidence of wealth in her house after her death. Fearing this could have been stolen along with some of the money the widow had held in trust for him, he turned to Tammy after he'd paid for his employer's funeral out of his own pocket.

The wily woman took him to the Churchyard at midnight on an agreed date after agreeing a considerable fee for her dubious services. During their time spent there Tammy cast a magical circle, utilised various herbs for protection and began to chant up the ghost of his friend. She went into the detail of all the apparitions she could see manifesting so well it seems that the poor chap took flight with fright unable to take his chances with the Devil and his nocturnal hounds as described by Tammy.

Now this chap had a cousin who felt that Tammy had duped his vulnerable relative so he himself took up the challenge to see Tammy and asked her to repeat the process with himself as witness. She agreed and a date was set, when the ritual was well under way a wailing sound emitted from behind the headstone of the deceased spinsters grave. A ghostly apparition rose up which the labourer's cousin allegedly fought to the ground only to discover, somewhat unsurprisingly, that it was none other than Tammy's husband James, in disguise. They confessed to their mutual illusion and deception but cut a deal with the cousin saying that he was to put the word out that he'd seen the ghost of the spinster and that she cursed any who owed her money or had stolen from her to do amends or else be haunted by her until their dying day.

This powerful psychological tool of paranoia served all parties involved quite well as the labourer gradually began to discover money and goods left in the night outside the house. This was thought to be by previously guilty parties over a period of time after the séance. He discovered the real will and money hidden in the thatch of the house at a later date.

Although Tammy's reputation was for the most part a benevolent one, one can see evidence of her deviousness and in one account she actually cursed her shoemaker for pestering her for payment. His business took a turn for the worse after this.

Her own life took a curious turn when she had to deal with her second husband's bi-sexuality and lessening support for their work but even from her death bed people still came to her for cures and she continued to assist them, almost until her dying breath.

She died aged 63, having turned her life from rags to riches but her grave is not known or marked.

For me, the name Joan Wytte is synonymous with the Boscastle museum of Witchcraft as only until relatively recently her skeleton was housed here but her story began in much earlier times.

Figure 6. Memorial stone to the memory of Joan Wytte, the fighting 'fairy' Woman of Bodmin. Photo courtesy of Graham King, Museum of Witchcraft, Boscastle.

She was born in Bodmin in 1775, a tiny lady of sweet nature by all accounts. It's thought that she was either a weaver or yarn twister but it is equally possible that, like other members of her family, she had entered into the leather business which was in its heyday at her time. She was known for her psychic powers from quite a young age and people began to seek her out for her prophetic skills. She practised a very common and indeed ancient practise of making offerings to the spirit of her local well often leaving '*clooties or yawns*' which were strips of material taken from her clients clothing and hung on nearby trees, especially hawthorn. The idea being that as the strips rotted away so would any ailment the afflicted person had. Of course many things can heal in time anyway but it's interesting to note that a more recent analysis of the water from this well showed up high levels of natural fluorides.

Ironically for Joan, and in spite of her predilection for healthy waters, by the age of twenty or thereabouts she developed a nasty infected abscess in her gums. The resulting pain and toxins that invaded her system turned this once demur woman into an angry, intolerant, bad tempered one.

Her clients still came to her but it wasn't uncommon for her to loose her temper and scare them off with her cursing and indeed it is recorded that her nocturnal audible emissions lead locals to think the Devil himself was visiting Joan in her bedchamber.

Things came to an unpleasant head when one night she picked a fight with several locals, even managing in her temper to airlift some of them with her extraordinary strength. Their injuries were severe enough to lead to her conviction for brawling and serious assault and subsequent imprisonment in Bodmin gaol.

Poor Joan was now imprisoned in dreadful conditions and forced to work the treadmill for hours at end. She eventually succumbed to bronchial pneumonia and died at the age of 38.

For us, this story is perhaps one of the most tragic. Toxic shock can completely change a person's temper causing irritation, intolerance, fear, anxiety. It can cause a high fever at times and kill through contracting septicaemia but thankfully these days people can be cured of it by modern medicines. The incredible strength associated with it is also a common one.

Even well after her death Joan's physical remains became quite remarkable in themselves. A surgeon who moved to the area soon after her demise made friends with the gaol doctor, who told him tales of Joan's incredible strength. He had kept a death mask of the woman and her corpse was still resting in the mortuary. The surgeon wished to acquire her remains for research but the gaol governor had other plans for her skeleton and instead decided to utilise it as a focal point for a night of medium-ship or séance. The evening didn't go as planned though and it's alleged that Joan made her presence felt by attacking those holding bones to create false rapping noises causing her coffin lid to blast open with such a degree as to terrify the audience who ran for cover. Her bones returned to the medical store room until 1927 when the prison closed and a doctor in north Cornwall acquired them and carried out a forensic autopsy on them.

It was via this doctor that her remains came into the hands of the original curator of the Witchcraft museum, a one Cecil Williamson. After much poltergeist activity in the museum and out of respect for the lady herself, her bones have since been buried in some woodland nearby in an unspecified location by the now owner and curator, Graham King.

A permanent memorial to her exists at the museum and reads:

> Joan Wytte
> Born 1775
> Died 1813
> In Bodmin Gaol
> Buried 1998
> No
> Longer
> Abused.

One of our personal favourite characters of the past has to be Dolly Pentreath. She was born in 1692 as Dorothy Jeffery although this is mildly debatable as there are records for two ladies with similar names with about ten years difference between them.

Much is made of how she didn't marry but had one child, a son named John. She made her living as a seller of fish, fortune teller and peller. She would buy the fish at Newlyn then walk it to places such as Castle Horneck to sell.

This didn't supply her with enough of an income though and although she had a reputation for being 'dirty about her person' and difficult to deal with, often launching into old Cornish when roused; she was still both respected and feared by members of her community. It was because of her reputation, as one of the few people left to speak the dialect, that academics with an interest in languages would seek her knowledge.

She actually stemmed from a much respected old family of the parish of St. Paul and her inherent magical knowings were, it's thought, hereditary.

One of the best stories told of old Dolly was of her encounter with a one Mr Price a local wealthy bombastic landowner

*Figure 7. An early woodcut study of Dolly Pentreath, witch and fish seller.
Probably drawn from life.*

who had the stupidity and audacity to literally cross her path one
day.

She, so it's said, was making her way slowly down a narrow
bridle path when Mr Price of Choon came upon her blocking
his way.

The silly and indeed inconsiderate man simply called out;
'*Clear the way!*' as he approached her from behind. The stubborn
woman remained resolute in her position on the path causing
Dolly the Spring, as she was often called, to shout obscenities
back to him at such an idea. Mr Price, having heard enough
insults from Dolly, then pushed his horse past her causing her
to lose the cowel of fish she was carrying.

At this Dolly became enraged and whilst hurling muddy fish
and stones at the rider cursed him in her native tongue shouting,
'*Cronnack an hagar dhu*' as she did so.

Mr Price knew of Dolly's reputation and was now feared of the woman thinking she'd placed a dreadful curse upon him so he offered to pay for her fish, an offer she immediately accepted. He then asked her of the curse she'd put upon him and what it meant. She asked for more payment, half a crown apparently, before she revealed her magic and said '*give the money first then and I must call you a fool for your pains*; (he gave her the money) *as all I said was to call you the ugly black toad that ye art*'.

Mr Price once realising she was mocking him threatened to horsewhip her for her trouble where upon Dolly countered back by threatening to rot his arm from its shoulder down, whilst intermittently gibbering in Cornish. This feared Mr Price enough that he rode off speedily, leaving Dolly to pick up what was left of her fish in peace.

So although her life was a hard one and she was a single mother, she used all the skills she had to bring up her son and to keep herself. She was still trudging up to three miles a day to sell fish until well into her eighties by all accounts. Never ever did she entertain the title of Witch preferring the more acceptable title of peller or *pellhe*.

She might well be the last accountable person recorded to have spoken fluent Cornish, a language thought to be similar, in sound at least, to Welsh. After her death at an age somewhere between 85 years and 102 (which is disputed) she was buried in the parish of Paul near Penzance and an epitaph was written for her both in English and Cornish it reads:

> *Coll Doll Pentreath cans ha Deau*
> *Marow ha kledyz ed Paul pleas*
> *Na ed an Egloz-hay coth Dolly es*
> *Bes ed Egloz-hay coth Dolly es.*

Or,

> Old Doll Pentreath, one hundred aged and two
> Deceased and buried in Paul parish too
> Not in the church with people great and high
> But in the churchyard doth old Dolly lie.

Sadly the epitaph never actually made it onto her tombstone; neither did her correct date of death but instead it says:

Here lieth interred Dorothy Pentreath who died in 1778
(she actually died 26th December, 1777)

One of the most famous names of the West Country that you may come across if enquiring about West Country Witches is that of Granny Boswell or as she was originally named Anne Boswell. Her family came over from Ireland during the potato famine like many others of the time and some chose the gypsy way of life living in horse drawn bow tops which had recently replaced the previous tradition of living in temporary benders. Born in 1813 of mixed Romanie and Irish blood she appears to have inherited many skills common to those who travel not least a greater understanding of people in general.

After years of hard farm labour she married an older man and by reputation somewhat of a character known locally in the Helston as 'King of the Gypsies' they had a traditional folk wedding including the custom of jumping the broomstick. She went on to give birth to no less than six children. Life was extremely hard for the family her husband worked the land as a labourer and developed rheumatic problems by the time he reached his early fifties a condition brought on by insufficient clothing and constant exposure to cold and damp conditions.

Having so many children to birth and bring up was difficult for Anne as she was unusual in that she left having children until her thirties and early forties.

But it was her magical abilities that people came to her for, she had the gift of healing by sympathetic magical means, prophecy or second sight, and even occasionally dealt a curse if paid enough or provoked.

On one such occasion she was stood in front of a particularly smart motor vehicle admiring it, it was ferrying voters on election day to the local polling station, she was somewhat inebriated at the time and was upset by the driver shouting and honking his horn at her to move, as a consequence she cursed that the car wouldn't make it to the end of the street. It didn't; a one inch steel rod snapped in two rendering the car useless.

She outlived her sons one of which ended up a convicted murderer and even well into her nineties she was still a force to be reckoned with. It's said she was very hard on her children often dealing out beatings and had a taste for boozing in the local pubs and that many of her clients were asking for protection from her magic or ill wishes as much as anything else but her life is still remembered today in the area as a powerful Witch and not one to mess with.

She had a gypsy funeral and all her jewellery and amulets were buried with her but as with all gypsy births and deaths she was born into the world in the fresh air and so she was taken outside just before she died. Her grave is at Tregerest near St. Just and can still be visited today.

An interesting story of little folk is found in the story of Anne Jefferies from St. Teath near Camelford. Born in 1626 to an impoverished family that one presumes couldn't afford to keep her she was sent to live with the slightly more prosperous and charitable Martyn family.

It is thought that her first encounter with the fairie realm occurred whilst she was ill so could have course been fever induced hallucinations but she insisted on having seen six of them, she claimed they fed her and refused to eat in front of others after this. From the description of her life recorded by Humphrey Martyn it appears she was a highly strung nervous young lady who the family protected from the news of her grandmother's death in 1646 for fear it might unhinge her. Just after this she developed epilepsy possibly as a result of distemper and was ill for some time often unable to stand and having fits that the family feared might finish her off. Once strong enough though she made a visit to the local church and it was significantly after this experience that she appeared to have gained the art of psychic healing.

One particular episode that she related directly to the little folk she saw was the time she healed her mother's leg. Her mother had gone to fetch flour from the local mill to bake bread but fell and twisted her leg. A passing neighbour heard her cry out, rescued her up onto his horse and took her home where upon Anne duly healed the woman's leg by simply stroking it with her hand. She revealed that she believed her illness had been caused by the fairies that had also told her that her mother wouldn't get far for putting Anne outside against her wishes that day and that they had given her this gift of healing also. News of this spread far and wide and people began to bring their sick and injured to her to receive magical healing. She was very successful by all accounts but never ever took any payment for her work.

Unfortunately her magic soon came to the attention of a local magistrate who accused her of being in league with the Devil. To which, Anne, virtually illiterate, quoted back the Bible at him saying:

> *'What, hath there been some magistrates and ministers to you, and dissuaded you from coming any more to us, saying we are evil spirits, and that it is all delusions of the Devil? Pray, desire them to read in the first epistle of St. John, chapter 4, verse one; 'Dearly beloved, believe not every spirit, but try the spirits whether they be of God'*

Sadly, John Tregeagle, a Justice of the Peace, arrested her and sent her to Bodmin gaol where she stayed for quite some time. Eventually the justice himself removed her to his own home where he put her claims of being fed by fairies to the test by starving Anne. It is also thought he harboured a secret fancy towards Anne himself and was indeed breaking the law by having her there. She was soon passed onto another branch of her adoptive family and took up residence in Padstow with Mrs Frances Tom, a widowed elder sister of her fathers.

She later moved in with the brother of Mrs Frances and soon after met her husband to be. Once married, she was left in relative peace to get on with her life but she continued her healing work and her claims of her special relationship with fairie folk.

A tale that is often re-told time and time again is that of the mysterious Lord and Lady of Pengerswick and the Witch of Fraddam.

Lord Pengerswick arrived in Cornwall having come from the East with a beautiful exotic woman who some described as a '*Saracen*'. The castle he built as their home was a closed shop to all but a few servants who were bound to secrecy outside its walls. But, people being people, some stories did escape including those telling of his occasional isolation for days on end burning strange herbs and oils and calling up spirits and demons whilst his Lady would play sweet music on her harp. It seems she, his Lady, was very much a bird in a gilded cage and he her enchanter and gaoler. His summoning and callings were often heard from outside the castle walls and neighbours linked this with great storms that often appeared to synchronise with his magic.

But he was also known for his generosity in the locality and his extravagance often outweighed the price of an object of his desire. So local people tolerated this man with his weird ways, it seems, as an occasional benefactor to the community.

His origins were murky, some say that he and his wife and servants, all came from Arabia. As did his stunning white horses which in his hands were obedient and docile but in the hands of others were virtually wild.

Now there was a local Witch who took umbrage with Lord Pengerswick, alleging that her spells were being thwarted by his magic incantations and she declared a magical war with him. She took herself to Kynance Cove and, it's said, called up the Devil, offering her soul in return for help in destroying Lord Pengerswick.

And so it's said, that about the time of the spring equinox when a great storm raged, the Witch boiled her evil brew to poison Pengerswicks' horse as it drank from a trough she placed near to a path she knew the Lord would soon travel. The witch sat nearby hardly able to contain herself with excitement of her deal with the Devil and the imminent arrival of Pengerswick. It wasn't long, allegedly, before she heard the horse and its rider approach, but the horse snorted loudly when it came upon the trough and the Lord, alarmed, lent over to his horses ears and whispered something to it where upon the horse kicked out at the hidden Witch and in so doing landed her in the very brew she aimed to poison the creature with. The Witch screamed out in terror but it was too late for her as Lord Pengerswick uttered his own spell and magically the trough became her coffin, a whirlwind arose with the Devil in the middle of it and cast the coffin, Witch and all, out into the sea. Lord Pengerswick is thought to have stated: '*she is settled till the day of doom*' before riding off into the night.

Since then there have been many sightings of the Witch of Fraddam out in her coffin bobbing on waves, stirring up storms, using her crock as a paddle. It is said that only the ghost of Lord Pengerswick is able to calm her by blowing his trumpet three times from high on the cliffs to silence her wicked ways and calm the seas.

We haven't heard or seen the Witch of Fraddam but Gill might have had an encounter with Drakes drums. Francis Drake isn't a

Figure 8. Marchant's Cross marks a branch of the Abbott's Way along which Drake hunts the Wish Hounds.

name normally associated with Witchcraft but he was known to utilise drums occasionally to call up winds to his own end. He originated from Devon and kept his strong Devonian accent throughout his life in spite of his travels far abroad and frequent visits to Queen Elizabeth I's court. He was described as both warrior and Witch by Ursula and Roy Radford who say he also employed the use of charms and spells throughout his life. Seeing as he came from a humble country background rich in folklore and charmer's, one can understand how this came to pass.

Gill's odd experience:

I had occasion to spend a night in the Wellington Hotel in Boscastle, in early May 2004. Although it's not a place synonymous with Drake I was kept awake until well past midnight by the sound of persistent drumming coming from outside. The next day I visited the Witchcraft museum and asked the owner, Graham King, if he'd heard the drums. He said not and was surprised as he himself had been in the Wellington that evening until quite late, but I have no other explanation for what I heard there and it was loud enough, I thought, to wake the whole town. If anyone else heard this or has a rational explanation for it, I would love to hear from them.

Another tale of Drake's supposed Witchcraft is linked with the village of Stogumber in Somerset where he is better known for his magical interruption of a wedding. Drake was engaged to be married to an Elizabeth Sydenham but she called it off and declared her betrothal to another man. On the very day of her marriage a great thunderclap and storm hit the party as they approached the church. A huge cannonball was thought to have fallen at the bride's feet causing her such fear as to call off the wedding and later marry Drake upon his return from sea. This cannonball, or meteorite, is kept at Coombe Sydenham House.

Two modern day charmers listed in Rose Mullin's book *White Witches a Study of Charmers* are Ivan Miners from Lostwithiel and

Figure 9. Bucland Abbey – Sir Francs Drakes's old home.

Joan Bettison who resides on the edge of Bodmin Moor. Ivan comes from a long line of Cornish charmers, he doesn't normally take any payment for his healing and has quite a reputation for being able to magically knit bones and stem bleeding (once enabling a local chap who had several bad cuts to his fingers to get to hospital without loosing blood causing a bit of a surprise once he arrived at A&E for treatment). The power to stop bleeding is a common ability to charmers with those from the Zennor area being perhaps the most prolific.

Joan has inherited skills from both parents which is considered unusual for it is usually only along one line that the tradition is passed on. She descends from a family of charmers that once lived on the Isles of Scilly. Up until 1962 she carried out the local postal delivery often being stopped on her journey at various houses and asked to perform various charms and healing, from animals to people. She still reads the tea leaves and cures ailments until this day.

A very novel but much older tale of Witchcraft from Kingsbridge in Devon tells of two neighbours who were about to set off for a walk when a storm blew up. Fearing they would get wet they decided to wait a bit and have some lunch instead, agreeing to call for one another later. One of the neighbours returned home and fancied some pancakes. As an accomplished pancake maker she set about mixing her batter, but nothing would go right, try as she might the batter kept curdling. As she glanced across at her fire she noticed a large black toad sitting there and in a fit of pique threw the contents and pan at it, presuming it to be the source of her problem.

The toad magically disappeared and after it had gone she managed to get her mixture right.

After the rain had passed she called for her friend who's daughter opened the door and informed her that mother couldn't come out as her mother was *'Taken suddenly bad in the face'* The pancake maker went upstairs to see her friend and found her in bed with a badly scalded face. As toads are linked to Witchcraft and shapeshifting magic, the neighbour was labelled as a Witch from then on.

Old Jane, a well known witch who lived in a village near South Molton in Devon, was being teased and tormented on a fairly regular basis by stone hurling youngsters who had nothing better to do. On one such occasion a young lad threw a sharp stone at her which struck her face causing it to bleed, she in turn lost her temper, quite understandably and cursed him thus: *'You threw that stone and you shan't speak again until I let 'ee'*

The young lad was subsequently silent for days, causing his mother to take the matter up with the local vicar, doctor and headmaster of the school. Their combined forces called Old Jane to account for herself. She turned up instantly, giving her tormentors mother the 'eye' and then demanded that the boy spoke by simply stating: *'Speak boy'*. She continued *'You know you can speak as well as I can, can't 'ee?'*

The little lad nervously replied *'Yes ma'am'*.

It's thought he retained quite a stutter after this incident but the meeting broke up in chaos. One hopes the young lad acquired better manners after this incident.

There was once an old lady called Charity who lived in a village near Axmouth in Devon. The locals believed she had overlooked or cast her eye at a man who then became ill. Nobody could cure him, so the village doctor took a trip to visit a White Witch some miles away for a consultation. The Witch, a man, told him that Charity had caused the affliction and he would punish her with nine days illness by his own magic which would only be broken by an old lady coming through the village crying. This happened and a visitor to Charity during the illness remarked that Charity seemed to think some spell had been cast against her but she couldn't understand why as she didn't think she'd wished or done any harm to anyone. The following day it was noticed that some of Charity's window panes had been smashed. Yet youngsters approached by a concerned villager recoiled in horror at the thought of offering to fetch a glazier to fix them as they believed it was Charity herself and her nocturnal broomstick activities that caused it.

The man who had consulted the White Witch used to be Charity's neighbour and claimed that in all the time he lived next door to her he'd never been able to keep pigs in his sty. They had all become agitated and over excited and worn themselves out unable to settle there even going so far as to claim they died of exhaustion so he'd given up on keeping any.

A woman who had attended Charity whilst she was ill swore she would never enter the house again as there was '*something uncanny about the old lady and the house*'.

She claimed there was a large box under the bed which Charity had forbidden her to open but she couldn't resist temptation and waited until the old lady was asleep to open it. Allegedly she found, to her surprise, that it was full of toads. How much of this is true though or the invention of over active imaginations wanting a scapegoat, is of course open to speculation.

There is a lovely little story of an enchanted Cocoa tin from Crediton in Devon. The tin contained many nails and was a present from a neighbour to his wood working friend. Once the nails had been used up, the tin began to develop a life of its own. No matter where the owner tried to keep it; in draws, boxes etc. it would still break free, often leaping up onto the ceiling before crashing down again. After a while, the owner of the troublesome tin took it to a White Witch believing it might be possessed of a spirit or worse still a curse from his neighbour who had long since moved away.

The Witch told him to take the tin to a deep pond at midnight on the dark of the moon and discard it out into the middle. He did as instructed whereupon the empty sealed tin sunk with a hiss and was never seen again.

Jessica Penberth, the co-writer of this book, originates from Helston and Feock and, as a successful psychic and reader of the Tarot, feels she owes her '*knowings*' to her Cornish lineage.

She has felt drawn to herbalism, kitchen 'witchcraft' and modern paganism throughout her life and her uncanny ability to accurately pin point people's troubles and aid their own cure without any prior information is common to those born of such a magical place, even if she now lives far away deep in the fens of Cambridgeshire.

I'll let Jessica take over here and give you her own feelings of what it is to be born with Cornish magic in your veins...

'Whenever I go home I feel like I've clicked into place somehow, as if I grow roots into the very ground, where I feel safe and secure. I feel I become part of the land and it makes my soul sing. The whole of Cornwall is such a spiritual place and I feel it in every rock, in the sea and in all the wildlife around me. It can be very wild down there too, it gives you a great sense of respect and awe to the power of Mother Nature when you see the waves crashing on the rocks at Penberth Cove and you see the mist rolling in from the seas and across the moors. Magic is in every nook and cranny that you look in, from the Holy wells and magnificent standing stones to the cairns and the quoits. Some of the hardest magic, that of changing yourself, I have manifested whilst sat quietly in the comforting arms of the quartz circles at the Merry Maidens and at Duloe. My heart belongs to St. Just and the Penzance peninsula. That is where I feel most alive and powerful, in touch with the earth and

everything around me, where I can see both forward and
backwards in time, where I feel my destiny lies. I hope to make
my home there one day with my husband David and my three
cats Freya, Tom and Lucy. Meanwhile I try hard to connect
with the spirit of the loci in the area in which I live now.
However, as it's meant to be underwater, being reclaimed land,
I don't find it as easy as connecting with the devas, spirits,
piskies and Gods and Goddesses of my homeland.'

Just like Jessica, many of the pellers and charmers of the West
Country both past and present would consider their skills more
divinely given than any supernatural gift. The origins of their
craft may well be rooted in older pagan practises but very few
of the pre-Twentieth Century practitioners would consider themselves pagan or wish to be given the label of Witch. The word
'charm' is a clue in itself as it originates from the old English
cyrm, meaning a hymn or carol, indicating that most would be
sung and/or repeated poetically. The Latin word *Carmen* also
links up with charm as it refers to the Goddess *Carmenta,* so
may well go back to the Roman times. It is thought to have
been a female adoration of this Goddess that provided the
charm or magic associated with her.

Many of these charms would end in words such as; 'in the
name of the Father, Son and Holy Ghost' as Christian appen-
dages to a formerly Goddess oriented form of healing magic.

As none of the pre-Christian charms have survived in written
word it can only be presumed that the charms themselves owe
something to the Goddess energy that was sought for help, but
that the Christian adaptation was added once peoples of the
area had converted to this religion during the 'dark ages'.

Many of the charms from medieval times onwards have survived and some can be found in our chapter on Ointments,
Charms and Spells.

Indeed right up until the Witch Hunting era of the Sixteenth and
Seventeenth Centuries our old folklore practices were pretty much
tolerated by the Church as long as they were with good intent.

Today's charmers and pellers continue this ancient tradition regardless of their religious beliefs, with both Christian and non-Christian practitioners available to seek help from, but the majority of today's self-proclaimed Witches and covens seem to have migrated to the Glastonbury area, Bodmin, Dartmoor and the north Cornish coast with other individuals dotted about the whole of the West Country.

Of Crime and Punishment

The Witchcraft Act was repealed in 1951, yes that recently, but it was replaced by the Fraudulent Mediums Act instead. By this, one presumes that nobody can these days be accused or charged with Witchcraft but can be taken to court for summoning the wrong spirit at a séance, both of which seem equally ludicrous.

It is interesting to note that although there were many Witchcraft charges and trials in the West Country, very few were actually convicted or hung as a consequence.

The majority of lesser charges appeared to be squabbles between women, especially under the influence of alcohol, or spiteful accusations between long standing rivals, or paranoid villagers looking for scapegoats.

More often than not, common sense prevailed in the West Country with most cases being thrown out of court or disproved in some way before conviction but if you were unlucky enough to find yourself guilty as charged you could expect to languish in gaol for quite some time in squalid conditions. Many didn't survive these internments and if they did, would be greatly weakened by the experience. Those hung were few but in order of severity let's look back in time and see just what could land you with a criminal charge, conviction or death sentence prior to the twentieth century.

We've already covered poor Joan Wytte of Bodmin but there is another tale just as dreadful to consider and this is the story of the Bideford Witches.

Temperance Lloyd, Susanna Edwards and Mary Trembles were all impoverished elderly women and thought to be members of a Witches coven in or near Bideford. By the time they were tried in 1682 Temperance Lloyd had already faced two previous charges of Witchcraft. Susanna Edwards confessed to have been recruited by the Devil himself at Parsonage Close where she met him allegedly dressed in black. Mary declared she was asked to join the coven by Susanna. This was the height of Witch fever in England and was a particularly ridiculous case with charges such as the Devil disguising himself as a cat and was seen jumping into the house of one of the accused at twilight. Another being that they were untrustworthy foreigners when in reality they were probably just Welsh in origin! The judge erred towards lenience in this case but the feelings of the locals was so venomous and overwhelming that confessions were extracted from the frail old ladies who, under such provocation and humiliation and torture like so many others before them, relented and agreed to anything cast against them. It was also noted that when being taken to gaol Susanna cast her eye at her gaoler who immediately had a fit or seizure.

Roger North wrote up an account of the trial and said: '*The women were very old, decrepit and impotent, and were brought before the assizes with as much fury of the rabble against them as could be shewed on any occasion. The stories of their acts were in everyone's mouth ... all which the country believed, and accordingly persecuted the wretched old creatures.*'

It was thought there would be a riot if they were acquitted so instead they were sentenced to death on 25th August, 1682.

A classic example of Witch fever and subsequent execution occurred in 1663 in Taunton in Somerset. Mrs Julian Cox was tried for bewitching a servant girl whom she had previously begged for money unsuccessfully from. The servant girl alleged that the beggar woman, Mrs Cox, had appeared to her in spectral form and coerced her into swallowing large pins against her wishes.

Other allegations were that she would shape-shift into a hare to send bad luck to the local hunt, a witness reporting he had actually seen this occur. He reported at the time: '*He knowing her was so affrighted that his hair stood on end; and yet spake to her asked her what brought her there; but she was so out of breath that she could not make him any answer.*'

She was also accused of using black magic against her neighbours cows who went mad and that she flew on a broomstick with another Witch and a 'black man' accompanied them.

At her trial she was asked to recite the Lords prayer, which she did but fatally omitting one crucial word. In the sentence 'and lead us not into temptation', she left out 'not'.

She was found guilty and executed.

The case of Mary Hearne took place at the Cornwall assizes on 27th October, 1927. The lady herself being 68 years old when charged. It came to light that Hearne had been supposedly treating a one Richard Harris Paddy for an illness he believed had come from being overlooked, a common occurrence of evil eye casting at the time. He had be-friended the gypsy woman and trusted in her abilities enough to give her regular sums of money to support her, the largest amount being claimed as £40, a considerable sum in those days. Hearne claimed at her hearing that Paddy had been like a husband to her for some twelve years, hinting at a possible sexual relationship between the two. He said she would use a compass and mutter strange incantations including mentioning planetary bodies such as Venus as she waved her hands over him in an attempt to heal him. It sounds as though this odd couple had some sort of falling out at some stage as Paddy relates to Hearne threatening to cause him blindness and even being taken to his bed. His employer became suspicious however and brought the whole episode out into the light resulting in Hearne being charged and found guilty, having to serve six months imprisonment for her troubles.

The Somerset Covens

Two notable covens were supposed to be practising during the 1660's, one at Wincanton the other at Brewham. The Wincanton coven is thought to have consisted of eight men and six women, not the normal association of the obligatory thirteen that we are more used to hearing of. Ann Bishop was named as being the head of this coven and it's said both covens were visited by the Devil, who peculiarly named himself Robin. One thinks there is more to this Robin than meets the eye, he could of course be a reference to the Horned God but we suspect he was the illusive manipulator of both covens and probably just as real as you or I. He was described as being short of stature, dressed in black and having a deep resounding voice. Two other members of the same coven are named as being Alice Duke and Elizabeth Styl.

The Brewham coven is reported as consisting of ten women and one man including several, we presume, of the same families as three were described as having the surname Warberton and another four the surname Green, other individuals named as; Margaret Agar and the man, Henry Walter.

Robin is said to have met up with both groups at specific times and locations to feast and revel in the open air whilst dancing and plotting revenge on enemies, even going to the extent of practising the dubious activity of sticking pins in wax figures, a practise common to the West Country but normally associated today with Voodoo. Many of the covens had strange tales to tell of their initiation rituals, many of which were held in Churchyards by Robin. Some include walking backwards round the church and having toads and other animals associated with Witches suddenly appear out of thin air. Elizabeth Styl went as far as to say she believed she had traded her soul to the Devil in exchange for twelve years of good luck and pleasure and had signed a pact to this effect in her own blood. The Devil, or Robin, had appeared, given her sixpence then run off as she declared, 'cheap at half the price!'.

Many of them admitted to using flying ointments and keeping familiars, including a hedgehog, cat and a black dog.

The local justice Robert Hunt wanted to bring these covens to trial and pursued them with vigour with the backing of Joseph

Granville, a former vicar of Frome, but Robert's superiors were not about to let him unleash an all out witch-hunt in the county and for some reason, quite unusually for the time, he dropped the case.

3

Modern Witchcraft in the West Country

There are still quite a few practising West Country Witches. We've already mentioned a couple of modern day pellers and charmers but there are those who openly describe themselves as Witches also. Most will claim a hereditary lineage, believing a Witch is born not made. It is the inherent genetic power of these mysterious people that affects the magic, not the substances, spells, rituals, tools or anything greater than these. A genuine Witch is supposed to have the ability to literally inflict his or her will out into the universe to gain the effect required. As magical enquirers and practitioners we find this interesting. Many Gnostics aspire to this as do most of the positive thinking 'New Age' movement. The rest of his or her actions are more for the benefit of those who seek her out. There does indeed seem to be an element of showmanship in Witchcraft and it isn't always easy to decide how the magic has been worked. Was it the spell, the charm, the materials used, the moon phase, the familiars? Or was it something far less sensational that being the belief of the person in the abilities of the Witch? This could be all the energy required.

We might not ever find out and in some ways we feel that this air of mystery should remain, if only as a reverent testament to the ancestors of all touched by Witchcraft.

We had the good luck to come across a modern practising Witch who originated from the town of Padstow but now lives in the heart of Somerset, near Glastonbury. Wendy would prefer not to give her real name as she is a solitary practitioner not keen to be inundated by curious folk who might just see her as a tourist attraction; she did however say this on the subject:

My mother was a Witch and her mother before her; I come from a long line of witches. I don't remember being taught my craft as witchcraft, it was just the way our family did things but we were told to keep many of these things secret. (We asked for an example from her past) When I was young I was being manipulated at school by this girl, she used me as her side kick, I began to dread going to school and soon my mother picked up on this.

She told me to invite the girl to tea one day, (she laughs here) I thought my mum had lost the plot, but I did as I was told.

Well the girl didn't turn it down, in fact to my surprise at the time she actually took me up on the offer and she agreed to come to our house, we lived in a little cottage in the heart of the town not far from the harbour.

My mum had made biscuits and her own home made blackberry juice for us to have after playing, I felt very uneasy and I didn't really know what to do with the girl but we played with dolls for a while. Of course this girl insisted on having the best doll to play with and the best clothes to change her into but I was still frightened of her so I let her have her way. We played in my room for a couple of hours then my mother called us downstairs.

I remember the biscuits, they were ginger ones shaped as hearts, she'd put one jelly tot on each one.

Well, we ate our biscuits and drank our juice and then my mother said it was time for the girl to go home.

I wasn't aware of any magic being performed or any spells being cast but after that day I didn't have any trouble with Carol and eventually we became friends.

Once I was old enough, my mother told me what she had done and it was so simple I found it hard to believe at first.

She said she'd invited her in genuine love, my mother had a huge compassionate spirit and could often see beneath a persons anger to the source, a gift I've thankfully since found within me too. I'm certainly less judgemental than I was when younger! Anyway, mum made the biscuits and blackberry juice in the name of the spirit of love and she opened the little girls heart to the potential of accepting generosity of spirit into her life.

It worked.

This was one of my first lessons in our craft, so I always give love first to any who come my way and keep a hospitable house but I also learnt how it can go wrong, magic I mean (We asked Wendy for an example)

When I was a bit older, about fourteen, a boy I knew was out chasing sea gulls. This wasn't unusual but the one he was going after was one we'd been feeding on our garage roof. The gull was just learning to fly and was pretty vulnerable. This particular day the boy managed to hit our sea gull, we called him Paddy, Padstow? Corny really! Anyway this boy was out with his catapult and hit the gull's wing. I was furious and flew, almost literally (she giggles) at him and as I did so I remember wishing the boy could feel that same pain! At that moment the boy screamed out grabbing his right arm, he looked right round at me and then this fisherman ran over to see what on earth was going on, but all I could think of at the time was helping Paddy. He squawked all the way home, he was heavy too, how I held onto him I'll never know. The next day the boys mother came to our house angry about what had happened demanding an apology from me. My mother asked me if I'd hit the boy. Of course I hadn't, so I said not.

The boy's mother was still not satisfied and accused me of lying. My mother asked me what happened, I told her the truth of it.

Then all hell broke loose with the boys mother, an ardent Catholic I might add, shouting: 'you're either a liar or a bloody witch!' I was shocked she swore.

My mother assured her I wasn't a liar but didn't deny the other, she just said maybe the boy hurt his own arm or was making it up.

I learnt a valuable lesson about controlling my temper and also about not always being so honest. Had I lied and admitted to hitting the boy, the mother would have still been angry but not accused us of Witchcraft and the boy would have been the only one other than myself to know the truth, but of course he did know and he always asked me if 'that were one of my birds?' before using his catapult after that. I had many birds (she tittered)!

These days I concentrate on healing and that's the main reason people come to me. I use a hands on method (I suppose you'd call it 'spiritual healing') and often find Moon and sea energies the most potent. I don't succumb to many of the modern practises, I don't feel it's part of my tradition and many of my methods are less than exciting. I have read many of the modern books on Witchcraft though, yes I have quite a collection now, but it's not for me. I work with who I see as the Moon Goddess and observe nature, birds especially. They tell me most of what I want to know. I suppose I am just a little eccentric but I can live with that. All my clients come to me through word of mouth, I don't earn my living from it, we usually barter something. My real work is bringing up my five children, it doesn't leave me much spare time for anything else!

We left it here as we felt Wendy was ready to move off the subject but she is a classic example of true hereditary Witchcraft and we both felt she certainly had something about her, as in an amazing zest for life and incredible energy which seemed to emanate from a very centred calm place from deep within her. She was also a great hostess and made us feel very welcomed in her lovely home. She showed us one of her mothers magical stones which by appearance looked just like any large pebble you'd find on the beach until she told us to look closer. There seemed to be a very rudimentary face etched into the surface, not intentionally as if by human hands, but almost as if the spirit of the stone was smiling through. She said her mother called it '*Happiness*' and would often lay it on someone if they were ill and nine times out of ten the person would recover soon after.

The practice of solitary Witch is perhaps the oldest and they are not too easy to find as even in these less prejudicial times people are still a little reticent about opening up or revealing any of their methods. There are some who have taken the other route and been brave enough to come forward openly as witches. Cassandra Latham is a West Country Witch who actually goes so far as declaring her trade as a professional Witch on her tax forms.

Then there are the covens that by their very nature prefer to retain a discrete distance from publicity, we've heard tell of one that used to be on Bodmin Moor and is exclusively a female coven of Goddess worshipping practice. They celebrate the Full Moon and other seasonal celebrations. A friend of our's was invited once to one of their circles one evening and said it was all taken most seriously and the Priestess of the coven insisted all had a bath or shower before leaving their houses as a form of ritual cleansing. They also dressed in special gowns or robes and were not to wear any underwear or artificial fabric. Our friend was leant one for the occasion. They proceeded to a stone circle, which involved quite a journey by all accounts, and once there the Priestess instructed all of them to join hands whilst she called upon the Goddess energy of the place and the energy of the Full Moon. Our friend said she felt a great rush of energy pass through her which she described as '*incredibly invigorating and magical, as if it had come out of nowhere*'. She also said the Priestess appeared to glow with a magical radiance. After this they then proceeded to chant and our friend said she was amazed at how easily she picked up the words and how the chant itself resonated, triggering something from deep within her. After this the Priestess gave their offerings, they each took something special that they were prepared to sacrifice to the Goddess. The Priestess had told them to bring something in advance and that it could be anything as long as it was 'of the earth' and not going to do any harm to either another person, animal or the environment. Our friend took a necklace. Once the offerings had been made the Priestess gave thanks on behalf of all attending and after one more chant they left for home.

Our friend said this was one of the most profound experiences of her life. The next day the Priestess took our friend to Men-an – Toll as she felt our friend needed to visit the stone and pass through it. She was told this was a common initiation for all who are invited to join the coven. She declined as she lived far away and couldn't promise to be a regular member but the Priestess encouraged her to pass through it anyway as it was stressed to her that her physical presence wasn't necessarily required and therefore from now on, and whenever she needed it, she could focus on the coven in her mind and be joined in spirit.

She says this has always remained a great strength to her in times of trouble and although they have lost touch with each other now she still remembers it as a most empowering experience.

One of the most commonly found forms of Witchcraft practised today is Wicca, a ritualistic religious path involving aspects of sympathetic magic that is difficult to trace accurately, other than to state that it definitely emerged publicly around the time of the second World War.

There are many names associated with the origins of this form of Witchcraft and many claims to initiating its conception.

If we trace back to the late Nineteenth Century, in 1888, we see the rise of the Hermetic Order of the Golden Dawn. This occult group owes its knowledge to many other groups such as the Rosicrucian societies, freemasonry, and theosophy.

A name synonymous with the occult world and mystery schools is Aleister Crowley, who was responsible for the founding of *Ordo Templi Orientis* (OTO) an offshoot of the Hermetic schools. This massive ego was obsessed with sex magic and drugs and although probably a genius in his own right, he and his friends were inadvertently instrumental in giving witchcraft a bad name yet again. He called himself The Beast and gave himself the number 666. He exposed many of the Golden Dawn and other Hermetic and Theleminite practitioner's secrets throughout his life and is probably most remembered today for taking St. Augustines quote: '*Love and do what thou will*' and altering it to read: 'love *is the law, love under will*' which subsequently became: ' *do what thou wilt an it harm none*' a common creed of today's Wiccans and some witches.

The modern Wiccan movement that subsequently evolved owes its origins not only to the likes of anthropologist Margaret Murray, museum curator Cecil Williamson, occultists Gerald Gardner, Aliestair Crowley, Doreen Valiente and Alexander Saunders to name but a few, but also to the mixing and blending of our native folklores, traditions, the Qabala, Freemasonry and practising covens and witches these people came across. By blending elements of all these subjects together we now have the most commonly practised form of witchcraft or magical religion Wicca and its derivatives.

They follow what they describe as the 'wheel of the year' and are meant to believe in a threefold law of karmic return, *i.e.* any magical practise will return upon the sender three times.

Most Wiccans today see the year as broken up into eight convenient segments; the eight point star that also corresponds with Venus the planet of love. The year ends on 31st October, with Halloween and the New Year begins on 1st November, this day corresponds with the old Celtic New Year. The next important date in their calendar is the Winter Solstice marking the shortest day and the return of the sun, on or about 21st December. The following date on the wheel is the 2nd February, marking the melting of snow and ice and the beginning of spring or Imbolc, another borrowed Celtic word. Next comes the spring equinox in March, on or about the 21st, marking the mid-point of spring and the female fertility season, a date often associated with Oestre, Goddess of ovulation. Then we have 1st May, representing the male fertility, and the West Country has many seasonal May Day festivities still held here in some West Country villages and towns. Then we go onto the summer solstice, or 21st June, and the longest day marking the symbolic death of the sun with shorter days to follow it is a day that draws many to Stone Henge in Salisbury each year to celebrate. After this comes 1st August, or Lammas, marking the start of the harvest time followed later by 21st September, the autumn equinox, and end of the harvest. These seasonal dates are normally acknowledged and honoured by celebratory rituals in some way by most Wiccans.

Many Wiccan practises include circle casting, a method of defining a sacred space within which magical ritual can be performed safely. It is interesting to note here that old English for church is *circe* meaning circle. Prior to the symbolism of the sacrificial cross taking president as the design basis for religious buildings, circles were thought to hold great power in our own spiritual past here in the West. Naturally the most obvious direct link must have been the circular shapes of both the sun and moon our most obvious heavenly bodies. There are several ways one can 'cast a circle'. One is to walk the circle clockwise whilst chanting an appropriate statement of intent to declare the space safe from harm and sacred within, many witches do this and some like to hold either a besom broom, sword, wand or athame (magical knife) whilst doing so. What they probably don't tell you at the time is that although the words themselves may hold some power and influence in the universe, with the added energy of those hearing the chant also believing in the power, they are also most probably visualising a protective light which will encompass the entire gathering. This light will be seen on the witches inner plane as a complete ball, above and below those stood in the circle. The cardinal directions of north, east, south and west are also aligned and it is seen in the magical world to be important to acknowledge each direction being both in line with the earth's poles and cross quarters. Each direction is associated with the four basic elements of earth, air, fire and water, and although in our scientific times we now know there are far more than these four I doubt many witches want to go to the bother of calling each one on the periodic table. Earth represents all that is matter on the material plane; air, all that is thought and communication; fire, all that is energy and passion; and water all that is emotion and love, in very basic terms. But there is more to elemental magical knowledge than this and it can cover an entire book if one wants to delve deeper. By standing one person at each quarter, the witch can invoke the elemental force associated with it. They normally have a physical representation of each element present also. The proficient witch can do this because he or she has spent much time meditating on each elemental force and has learnt when to recognise its presence when called upon, *i.e.* he or she has mastered the elements. This is part of the mysterious aspect of witchcraft and one that only those prepared to experience personally can ever hope to understand. If the witch is performing a solitary ritual then they will call upon each element in turn themselves and it works just as well, if not better sometimes. The presence of each fundamental element is supposed to add its own energy to the ritual and is often described as a 'guardian' or 'spirit' of each direction.

Once the circle is cast and the elemental energies called upon then the witch can take one of two roads, he or she can simply open up their own magical energy to add the spiritual aspect to the proceedings or call upon another presence to be in the circle. The vast majority of witches call upon ancient deities or local spirits, this is often the part of magical rituals that invokes fear in the uninitiated and has been the aspect that has lead to most of the paranoia and persecution of the past. Only a properly trained or inherently capable witch can do this as it requires the ability to open up ones own inner plane energy centres to activate spirit of any sort from the ether. Again, as with invoking elemental forces, this is another area that remains a mystery to those outside the craft and for those born without the obvious ability it can take years of training to achieve any sort of response.

The results can vary from gentle, subtle loving energy being perceived by those in the circle to dramatic reactions and sometimes actual physical manifestations. This is why many people fear witchcraft. Yet, in our experience, there is nothing to fear and neither of us have seen any evidence of evil or destruction being manifested during a ritual, this is why the circle of protection is cast in the first place.

Some witches have decorated altars similar to a church altar on which various offerings, candles, magical implements, *etc* can be placed. For many this remains *in situ* permanently in the home as a place of sacredness. Whilst it is true that our pagan ancestors did make live offerings to their Gods and Goddesses, and there is certainly evidence that witches of the past did similar acts in spell casting, these days it isn't generally considered acceptable behaviour. The majority of modern witches respect and revere nature, probably more so than their ancestors did, although we can't speak for all of them. That having been said, we haven't come across any that offer up live sacrifices on their altars.

But it has to be said that this mysterious image of cloaked people, standing around in circles with altars and their 'offerings', still to this day conjures up memories of Vincent Price films and other associated Hammer House horror concepts with virginal sacrifices or the like being carried out. It is true that, in spite of the repeal of the witchcraft act, many modern witches still to this day feel decidedly uncomfortable about being completely open about their activities. Not that the vast majority of them have anything to hide it's just that their behaviour still invokes fear in others.

It's true that some covens did and maybe even still do indulge in sexual congress under the belief that this primal energy was a gift to whatever God or Goddess they had chosen to call upon. These tales certainly made headline news in the sixties and seventies but most wiccans today don't involve themselves with such behaviour at their gatherings, or would wish to. They have learnt from the mistakes of the past and many found that relationships crumbled under such so called religious pressure.

Without exception all the Wicca based rituals we've attended since the late nineties have been informal, relaxed affairs, of seasonal celebration. They are open to all who come in peace and want to offer their thanks. They are no more shocking than a visit to your local church on a Sunday, the only exception being that they have all been held in beautiful outdoor locations.

There is no official set way of organising these events, each practitioner being unique in their practice. Most group or coven based rituals are decided democratically in advance but there are usually two who act as priest and priestess to represent the male and female divine energy, as reflected in nature. For those of you who maybe curious to see an example of a Wiccan ritual, we've set out an example you can read later on. But it must be emphasised that this is only a basic simplistic ritual and some can be longer or more complex. The underlying emphasis of belief in divine spirit and acceptance of equality of God and Goddess, who are venerated and worshipped either in solitary sense or group situations, does appeal to many who feel the past two thousand years have been rather male oriented.

The Wiccan movement seems to have adopted many ancient sites or spiritually traditional places in the West Country as some of their spiritual homes or pilgrimages. Many practising Wiccans can be found here. It could be said that Wicca is the only organised religion to have originated from England and it more or less began in the West and South of the country (give or take the odd disputed claim by Gerald Gardner that he alone started it in the New forest by being initiated into a coven by a Witch called Dorothy Clutterbuck, way back in 1939).

Interestingly, most modern Wiccans we've met abhor the use of illegal drugs and are not necessarily practitioners of sexual magic, but their modern rituals use a system, that in part, evolved from the likes of the OTO and the Golden Dawn.

Each Wiccan is an individual, so it is almost impossible to define all the beliefs and practises of these people on a separate basis.

A Group Wiccan Ritual

Various aspects of the ritual will have already been decided in advance of the day itself, such as location, time, parts for people to participate in, offerings, etc.

The particular group I know of, although not overtly Wiccan, take it in turns volunteering for the parts available, *i.e.* Priest/Priestess, calling the elemental quarters, casting the magical circle. To any onlooker unfamiliar with a Wiccan ceremony, this is what they are most likely to witness: The group will gather at a pre-agreed time and place, most probably an outdoor venue, either on common land or someone's garden. One group we know of has permission to bless an ancient meadow each summer solstice and a local farmers wife has created a permanent circle in her garden for use at other times of the year. It is a

Figure 10. Old woodcut of witch's flying.

popular misconception that all rituals are held at midnight. This is not true but some are and many are held at mid-day or evening as they are family events that all ages can attend.

People may choose to dress up for the occasion or not. Some groups insist on specific robes and cloaks, others don't, although the one we know of doesn't. The priest and priestess often wear something to distinguish them from everyone else, this might be a specific garb or just some leaves or flowers or other such appropriate head gear.

The group will arrange themselves in a circle with those calling on the elemental quarters in their appropriate directional positions, each with an example of the element they are calling. The priest and priestess are normally in the middle. An altar may have been prepared on which people can leave offerings, the group I've visited just lay flowers on the ground or under specific trees or wells.

The circle will be cast either by symbolically sweeping a besom broom around clockwise whilst making a declaration of the space as sacred and safe, or by the use of an athame, sword, staff or other such magical tool to the same end by the priest or priestess or specific circle caster.

Then the priest and priestess will make an opening declaration relevant to the day or season before the four people calling the elementals begin their summoning from north through east, through south to west, although some start in the east and work round clockwise.

The God and Goddess will be called upon by the priest and priestess either in unison or in turn and again the method involved can vary. Some like to hold their arms up and outward, looking up, some not. Any thanks, blessings, requests, *etc.* can now be made either by the priest and priestess on behalf of the whole group or, in the case of the one we know, they allow everyone to take turns in saying whatever they wish to the God and Goddess. This can vary considerably from the simple giving of thanks to a specific request either for themselves or someone else or the world as a whole. Some like to read out a poem or sing. As we say, each ritual is very different in structure with some more rigid than others. The offerings and their intent are given to the God and Goddess either individually or by the priest and priestess. Once all that has to be said has been said, the priest and priestess will give thanks to the God and Goddess before bidding them farewell and the same is done in turn for each quarter.

The circle can now be broken and most rituals end up in a picnic, feast, BBQ, party or something similar before people depart.

So where is the magic, you may ask? Well, it usually manifests after the event, *i.e.* anything asked for, normally happens. We have known rituals to deities such as Thor to produce some stunning, instantaneous thunder storms.

In our experience, regardless of religious path, spiritual awareness or definitive beliefs, the power of repetitive regular prayers or rituals, whether solitary or group oriented, often lead to miraculous experiences that can enrich us spiritually, emotionally, mentally, energetically and physically, both within and without.

What ever your beliefs may be.

Blessed Be. (A common respectful acknowledgement between Wiccans they also use Merry Meet, Merry Part and Merry Meet Again which goes back to Saxon times.)

Hedge Witchcraft

One of the contemporary Pagan paths that we are most interested in is that of the hedge witch or kitchen witch. This comes from the traditional idea of the village witch or cunning folk who practise alone, without a coven. The hedge witch is likely to worship the God and Goddess and practise spell craft for healing purposes and they may well teach the mysteries. This is unlike the traditional village witch who may well have not worshipped the God and Goddess and who may not have limited their expertise to just, good magic, as described earlier.

Today's hedge witch will be well versed in nature, may well be skilled in herbalism and proficient in the casting of spells and the ways of the Craft and it is more than likely that they will observe the Pagan seasonal festivals. The term hedge or kitchen witch refers to the traditional image of the witch living at the outskirts of the village and going through the hedge that surrounds the village or using items that grow in the hedge for their spell work, which was most likely carried out in the kitchen.

We like this somewhat romanticised view of witch craft and find that it helps to describe what Jessica does quite well. My kitchen at home is painted a beautiful red with sage green cupboards and it is around the kitchen table where I do my magic. A place where knowledge can be gained, gossip shared and broken hearts mended over cups of aromatic tea. In fact some of this book was written at that very table. This is a place of real magic where natural ingredients have been grown with care, in the garden, just outside the door, lovingly collected and hung to dry in the kitchen, scenting the room as they do so. It is at the oven, instead of the hearth, where I stand with my cauldron, a beautiful stainless steel stock pot. Here I transform these gifts from nature into food, drinks, lotions, potions and magical charms. This is the stuff of life.

I have a thriving herb garden which is split into two, one for culinary herbs and the other for medicinal herbs. These are used for making herbal teas, tinctures, decoctions, scented oils and vinegars, or they are just used to spice up supper. I also have a thriving vegetable patch and nothing beats going into the garden and picking the ingredients for lunch. Growing vegetables also makes you very aware of the seasons and what is happening in nature, which I feel is all part of the path I walk.

Spell craft is very important to me and I will use cord magic, candle magic, crystals, simple meditation or guided visualisation to help others. I enjoy making amulets and charms, and symbols are of great interest to me. I use divination to help myself and others and converse naturally with Spirit, helping to bring comfort to those whose loved ones have passed over. All of this feels very natural to me and is extremely fulfilling, so I am happy to wear the mantle of hedge witch and hope one day to be the wise woman of the village.

Although Jessica has put it very well, I'd like to add this: The Hedgewitch craft is very much a magical connection with the *genus loci* that is the ability of sensing the local spirits (be they of trees, plants, flowers, wells, paths, fairie circles, buildings or anything that is in the immediate vicinity of the witch). She takes her power from that which is around her and gives back by showing love and reverence to her local environment also. It is from this basis that our more recent understanding of conservation comes that of acting locally and affecting globally if we all partake of this premise. The Hedgewitch cares for her space. It nourishes her, both on an earthly plane and spiritually, so it pays to encourage this relationship and greatly enhances the place he or she occupies. Jess' garden reflects this well, it has a lovely benevolent atmosphere. It is good humoured with happy and well cared for plants, trees and herbs. Her environment is benefiting from her spiritual relationship with it and it shows!

Ointments, Charms and Spells

Author's disclaimer:

> Before anyone takes it upon themselves to emulate or put into practise any of these ointments, spells or charms it must be stressed that we cannot take any responsibility for the outcomes. These are intended for information only and some of the recipes may well be toxic or harmful were you to ingest them or apply them. Those we believe to be especially dangerous so are marked with a bold T for toxic. Those considered less dangerous are marked with a bold C, indicating caution should be used. Those we consider harmless are marked with a bold S for safe, if following instructions.

Flying Ointments

Before mounting their broomsticks witches first had to anoint themselves or their sticks with flying ointment, a vile concoction that may have included hallucinogenic and/or toxic ingredients. The use of toxic ingredients may well indicate that these ointments were not ingested, instead they would be placed upon the broom and then the witch would ride the broom allowing absorption through the skin which would allow the ointment to enter the bloodstream without having to be processed by the liver. If the witch was inside the house she would supposedly rise up through the chimney. Whether the witch physically flew out or not is obviously debatable but certainly some of the herbs and ingredients would induce some sort of trip for the user!

We have found various recipes for flying ointments:

C
2 parts Dittany of Crete
2 parts cinquefoil
2 parts mugwort
2 parts parsley

Add the herbs to fat to create the ointment and anoint to broom or body prior to attempting astral projection. I don't think we need to say where!

Or

C
4 drops sandalwood oil
4 drops jasmine oil
2 drops benzoin oil
2 drops mace oil

Add oils to beeswax/base oil and use as above.

Or

C
$\frac{1}{2}$ tsp. clove oil
$1\frac{1}{2}$ tsp. chimney soot
$\frac{1}{4}$ tsp. dried cinquefoil
$\frac{1}{4}$ tsp. mugwort

$\frac{1}{4}$ tsp. thistle
$\frac{1}{4}$ tsp. vervain
$\frac{1}{2}$ tsp. tincture of benzoin

Add oils to beeswax/base oil use as above.

If indeed you are tempted to try the ones above we suggest you use the ointment very sparingly to begin with as it is entirely possible your skin may react adversely to the ointment. It's probably best to put a small dab on your hand to start, if no reaction occursthen you should be alright, but skin elsewhere is more sensitive.

T

The ancient witch's flying ointments were a dangerous herbal concoction producing psychedelic effects. It consisted mainly of, parsley, water of aconite, polar leaves, soot (sympathetic magic, as they flew out of the chimney), bats blood (a herb, not the animal), deadly nightshade (*Belladonna*), henbane and hashish. Tradition has it that these ingredients were mixed together in a cauldron over a fire with the melted fat of an unbaptised infant, allegedly. Though this was more likely to be the residue fat that happened to coat the cauldron from last nights stew! This ointment did induce incredible hallucinations, psychic visions and astral projections.

Stories also abound in the West Country of witches using kites to fly and one such tale tells of a witch who would fly her kite deliberately over the chimney of a person's house when the smoke was rising to draw the energy of that house and its incumbents to her.

Ancient Witches Ointment
T (extremely toxic)
Cinquefoil, parsley, aconite, belladonna, hemlock and cowbane.

We decided not to give the exact quantities required as this one is far too dangerous to try at home.

Another Ancient Witches Ointment
T (Potentially Deadly)
Hog's lard, hashish, hemp flowers, poppy flowers and hellebore.

It's quite surprising to realise that the cauldron, or Witches pot, was often the only one in the house and would have been used for everything. Oils, tinctures, cooking and even these potentially dangerous flying ointments.

Often in Cornwall and the coast of Somerset and Devon witches were thought to cause storms at sea by dumping the contents of their cauldron out at sea.

Banishing Ointments

A banishing ointment could be procured from a Witch to aid a person who wants to rid themselves of unwanted attention, ill-wishing, illness, melancholic states of mind, and anything really that a person might feel is having a negative effect on their lives.

S

Ointment for melancholy, topical application only, not for internal use
$\frac{1}{4}$ tsp. fish oil (mackerel thought best)
1 tsp. St. Johns Wort
$\frac{1}{2}$ tsp. ginger
1 tsp. nutmeg

Blend into melted beeswax or base oil and allow to set.

Apply as and when required to inside of wrists or crook of elbow.

This one made us laugh as one can easily see how deliberately smelling even slightly of fish would be enough of an incentive to recover rather quickly, but there is modern proof that Omega 3, a derivative of fish oil, is both good for the heart and can lift mild depression. And although we haven't actually tried this one, we presume the more pleasing aromas of the other ingredients would mask the less pleasant smell of the fish oil.

Ointment or incense for banishing ghosts or calming restless spirits

S

1 tsp. mint

$\frac{1}{2}$ tsp. rosemary

$\frac{1}{2}$ tsp. sage

$\frac{1}{4}$ tsp. Frankincense

Grind all ingredients and add to melted wax or oil, can be applied to third eye area, up between eyebrows, or on each corner of the afflicted house, the dry ingredients can be burnt on the fire or charcoal as a banishing incense.

General banishing ointment

T

1 tsp. ground rosemary

1 tsp. ground bay leaves

$\frac{1}{2}$ tsp. ground rowan berries

$\frac{1}{2}$ tsp. myrhh

$\frac{1}{4}$ tsp. dragons blood

As per the above, grind to powder and add to oil or melted wax, apply with extreme caution. Not generally recommended as rowan berries are toxic.

Attraction Ointments

These have the opposite effect and will draw that wish you want to you providing you really want it that is and as with anything we wish for we should exercise some pre-thought or meditation as the old adage goes: 'Be careful what you wish for it might just come true!'

Love Ointment

S

Handful of dried rose petals

Handful of dried hawthorn leaves

7 drops of jasmine oil

5 apple pips

Grind all ingredients in pestle and mortar, add to melted beeswax or base oil, apply small dab daily to heart area for the three days leading up to a full moon, especially potent in May. (It is generally considered bad form these days to enchant particular people's affections and therefore we advise this is only used to draw love to you in a non-specific way.)

Clairvoyance
C
$\frac{1}{4}$ tsp. rue
4 drops cypress oil
$\frac{1}{2}$ tsp. frankincense resin or $\frac{1}{2}$ tsp. of oil
4 drops of pine oil

As per the above but apply to third eye area before needed.

General Good Luck
S
7 basil leaves dried
4 drops of lavender oil
7 sage leaves preferably purple dried
3 cloves
$\frac{1}{4}$ tsp. Nutmeg

As above can apply to body in sensible places *i.e.* wrists like a perfume, or to places you want to increase luck to *i.e.* front door of house, purse etc., within reason.

Amulets and Talismans

The cunning folk were often called upon to make talismans, amulets and charms for the village folk to protect them and for specific purposes. Here is a definition of the differences between these three items, which is very subtle but none the less it was important for the cunning folk to pick the appropriate one for the user.

Talisman

Talismans are objects designed to give specific power, protection, encouragement and energy to those who wear or own them. The important thing to note is that talismans always provide specific benefits to their owner and are usually made for specific purposes. Talismans can be made from almost any material, though they are frequently made of metal, stone or parchment and are inscribed with words or pictures. They are often made at spiritually and cosmically significant times to help provide extra power and energy. The most powerful ones are those that are made by their owners. They can be made for both positive and negative purposes, although one would not want to make a deliberately negative one for you.

The earliest talismans were natural. Primitive people would have used objects made from parts of animals such as a kestrel feather, shark tooth or snake skin, providing power and protection to the wearer. A necklace made from the teeth of a predatory animal is intended not only to provide protection but to also give the wearer some of the qualities of that particular animal that the teeth belonged to, *i.e.* someone wearing beaver's teeth would become industrious whilst someone wearing shark's teeth would become strong, fierce and energetic.

Amulets

Unlike talismans, amulets are intended for more general purposes and usually provide protection from danger. They can also ward off illness, ill-fortune or protect against ill-wishing. While talismans are active, amulets are passive, reacting to what is happening currently in the wearer's life. Originally amulets consisted of natural objects 'lucky' rabbit's feet (more lucky for the owner than the rabbit) and four-leaf clovers are examples of such amulets. Manmade objects have since become amulets especially in the form of body adornments, jewellery is still frequently used as an amulet. An amulet can also be specifically made for you to carry for protection.

Lucky charms

Lucky charms combine the qualities of both amulets and talismans. They are active like talismans and generalised like amulets. Charms are intended to attract good luck and good fortune to whoever owns them. Originally, charms consisted of words that were either spoken or sung. The word 'charm' itself is derived from the French word '*charmé*', meaning song. When people began writing the words instead of saying them, charms became associated with magical objects like amulets and talismans.

As you can see it is sometimes difficult to say if a certain magical object is a talisman, amulet or lucky charm. The cunning folk may well have used one object to perform all three functions, a lot depending on the belief of the person they were making it for. Essentially talismans provide active power, amulets provide passive protection and charms attract good luck and provide protection from bad. To the cunning folk it probably made no difference what they were called, the important thing was to understand what the person needed help with and find an object that would work for them.

The ancient Egyptians had four words that could be translated as 'amulet', all of them come from verbs that mean to guard or to protect. The word 'amulet' comes from '*amuletum*', Latin for 'an act which averts evil'. People began wearing amulets because of a natural desire to protect themselves in the often frightening world in which they found themselves. Amulets provided them with protection for the home, family and livestock. They protected the user from enemies that were natural or otherwise, most crucially they provided protection from ill-wishing and the evil eye. When the concept of Gods or a God became accepted, the Gods were often credited with providing the protective qualities that amulets render. Subsequently saints have been employed with the most popular, a well known one being St. Christopher, patron saint of travellers.

Certain amulets have stood the test of time and have become well known because of the benefits they provide. Obviously, if these amulets failed to provide the desired results they would have been forgotten long ago. Wearing or carrying an amulet harms no one and a familiar, trusted amulet provides pleasure as well as protection.

The acorn has been used as an amulet since druidic times. The druids worshipped in sacred groves of trees and the druids celebrated an oak festival at the time of the summer solstice. Many civilisations have venerated the oak and its acorn. The oracle at Dodena, in ancient Greece, was situated in an oak forest, the priests and priestesses would listen to the sounds of the trees and interpret them. The breezes in the branches were amplified by large bronze vessels that vibrated in the wind. In Scandinavia, the oak is related to Thor, in India to Indra, in Greece to Jupiter and in Finland to Ukho. The Romans made crowns of oak leaves to symbolise bravery and courage. As well as being a protective amulet, the acorn is considered a charm to attract good luck and a long life. Some people place acorns on window ledges to provide protection for the occupants of the house.

Anyone who, as a young child, or has young children will know, looking through Granny's button box is a magical adventure. Today, we consider buttons to be purely functional items but buttons were in use before button holes were invented. Buttons were originally considered to be both good luck charms and amulets, and they were exchanged as gifts, a custom I personally would like to see resurrected. Attractive buttons still make effective amulets, especially if they are given to you by someone who cares for you. There are a number of superstitions about buttons; it is considered bad luck to put a button in the wrong buttonhole accidentally. The remedy is to take the garment off completely and put it on again. Finding a button is considered fortunate (like picking up a penny) and means you will shortly make a new friend. If you are unwell and believe that the illness is caused by ill-wishing you should leave a black button where someone else will find it and thus you pass the ill-wishing on, although we are unsure on the karmic return of this practice?

A belief that appears around the world is that knots can catch evil spirits. A knot acts as a protective amulet that discourages evil spirits. Oddly enough the clerical dog collar is derived from the belief that the knot in a priest's tie could get caught up with an evil spirit that could cause mischief during church services.

In the West Country there is an old tradition of sailors arriving in a new port asking the locals to 'buy the wind'. This was achieved by knotting a rope with a stone and a gulls feather attached to it. This was tied to the mast and a suitable price paid to whomever did this act for them. Another interesting discovery connected with fishermen includes a witch known as Janie Rowe of Penzance. She utilised a bottle half filled with mercury to predict the weather well before the official invention of barometers or thermometers and to those asking for her foresight it must have seemed powerful magic indeed.

Parik-tils or blessing holders are used by Romany Gypsies. They contain a variety of small items such as coins, acorns, herbs, stones, feathers and pieces of paper containing spells or words of wisdom. Anything at all can be placed in the bags as long as it seems appropriate for the purpose that the bag was made for. Bags could be made as amulets for protection against unseen forces or the evil eye, or any form of ill-wishing and negativity. The bags could also be made as talismans to attract health, love, prosperity and longevity. The finished bags are charged by passing them over a candle flame before sprinkling them with water. A few droplets of perfumed oil can be added and it is then ready to be worn.

No one knows how or when talismans were first devised. However, they probably date back to the Stone Age. Paintings on cave walls show oxen, deer and other animals, which as described before is a type of sympathetic magic. By depicting animals on the walls of the caves early people were using symbols to attract prey to them. The first talismans were natural items such as stones or bones that happened to be a shape which reminded the finder of a particular animal or god or ability or characteristic of them. Other items were crudely carved to represent various deities.

As people became more skilled at making them, talismans became more elaborate. Small carved figures of ivory, pottery and metal dating from Palaeolithic and Neolithic times still survive today. No matter how simple or detailed they happen to be, people believe that talismans are imbued with the power of whatever it is they were made to represent.

During the crusades, many soldiers carried stones carved with runes to act as talismans. These rune stones had two purposes, to provide protection and to ensure success in battle. Soldiers of this period also carried bloodstones with them. Bloodstone is associated with Mars, the god of war and soldiers believed these stones would make them brave in battle as well as provide protection. They also believed that these stones could staunch bleeding and they were frequently bandaged against wounds to help the healing process. It is interesting to think that jewellery worn purely for decorative purposes was not known prior to the time of the French Revolution, before then jewellery was worn for only two purposes; either to signify high social standing or as a talisman.

The word 'talisman' comes from the Greek word '*teleo*' which means 'to consecrate'. Talismans are magical items that must be endowed with their power in some manner. In other words, talismans are charged to provide power and energy to enable them to achieve their tasks. They are usually made and charged at specific times to provide them with the essential energies they need to do their work. Without charging, a talisman cannot perform its specific function.

Everyone wants to be lucky. Throughout history people have carried lucky charms with them in the hope that it will make them more attractive, more intelligent and bring them more wealth and good fortune. People believed that misfortune could be caused by malevolent spirits so people in the community would go to the cunning person who would be able to neutralise the evil spirit by reciting or singing chants or songs. Solid objects became used as charms and are intended to bring good luck, a person's wealth or status have no bearing on this. Almost anything you care to imagine has been worn or carried as a good luck charm at one time or another.

Horse shoes are classic lucky charms; although you can buy a horseshoe it is much better to find one. Traditionally, a horse shoe should hang above the front door to ensure that good luck stays inside the house. The crescent shape of the horseshoe is considered protective. It is also believed to deter witches and the devil, this may be due to seven nails being used to secure them and seven is considered a spiritual number. There are two schools of thought as to which way up the horseshoe should be. Some say the curve should be at the bottom so that the luck is held within it, others say that the curve should be at the top so the luck drops down on you.

The rabbit's foot is a charm that symbolises fruitfulness and good luck. The good luck element comes from the belief that rabbits are born with their eyes open and this gives them power over the evil eye. The hind legs of a rabbit touch the ground before the front legs, this used to be considered unusual so they credited the back feet with magical powers. A rabbit's foot charm should always be kept in the left pocket. Traditionally, and funnily enough, the best rabbit's foot charm is one that contains the left hind foot of the animal that has been killed by a cross-eyed person on a full moon. One wonders how on earth this superstition originated!

There is an example of a charm bag in Dawlish museum that contains three bumble bees. It is described as one to bring health, wealth and happiness to its owner.

A treasured object that someone has given you makes an extremely powerful good luck charm because of the personal associations it provides. Most charms are purchased ready made but they can be hand made. As with talismans, making your own lucky charms provides a great deal of additional power and energy. Charm bracelets are still popular and allow the owner to wear many different charms at the same time. Charms can be worn or simply carried with you; they do not need to be visible to be effective.

Spells and charms

The traditional Guernsey worn by Cornish fishermen were highly personalised, magically protective items of clothing. Each family had its own pattern, with a special meaning and each individual had their own variation. This is thought to be so that a drowned man could be identified even if the body had been in the water for some time. The magical protective powers within those patterns, suited to the individual within the context of the family's pattern, was a means of keeping someone safe from the perils of the sea.

It is also common knowledge that the miners used to leave some of the crust of their pasty down the mines for the knockers, a form of piskie, by way of currying favour with them so that they would look after and warn the miners of any dangers. So it might be an idea, if you don't want to get into any trouble whilst you visit Cornwall, to leave a bit of pasty crust for the piskies.

Won't leave home spell for your pet

In the case of the feline, this spell could be construed as cruel but for wandering dogs and other domestic animals prone to straying it has its uses. Hold your pet up before a mirror, if it seems to notice its reflection it will remain at home. Or, if you have a fireplace, have the animal look up the chimney. This spell is best performed on the day that the pet arrives.

The most logical and powerful spell is simply to feed your pet properly and give it love and attention. This weaves a magic spell that is powerful enough to guarantee your pet's continued presence in your loving home.

Harmony at work spell

If things are getting a little hectic at work and your colleagues 'tempers' are getting a little frayed, offer to make everyone a drink, a cup of tea or coffee. When preparing everyone's drink stir each cup three times in a clockwise direction and say:

> May love, peace and harmony enter this work-place

You'll be amazed how effectively this simple spell works.

Spell for moving home

Tuesday is named after the god Tiw and is a day of action; this is a day auspicious for matters regarding prosperity, truth and new beginnings, so it is a good day to start a spell for moving home. On a piece of paper write down all the things that you would like to have in your new home *i.e.* number of bedrooms, off road parking, peace and tranquillity etc. Think very carefully about this as it is important. Place the piece of paper under a brown candle which is anointed with basil oil. Light the candle on a Tuesday and say:

> Candle as you burn tonight
> Let our new home come into sight
> Somewhere we'll be happy and gay
> Safe and sound no matter what may

After an hour or so blow out the candle. Repeat the process every Tuesday until you get your ideal property.

Charm for clearing hurt

Friday's New Moon is the perfect time to clear away any emotional baggage you may have been carrying from a previous relationship. Take a bowl of water, two pink candles which have been anointed with rose oil, one white candle and place on a table. In between the candles, in a safe container, burn some of your favourite incense. Sprinkle some salt into the water, ring a small bell and say aloud:

> Hurt and pain are banished tonight
> Fill my heart and home with light

Ring the bell again and throw the water out of the front door where it will drain away along with any emotional baggage.

Charm for mental and emotional well-being

On a Thursday night take a blue candle and anoint it with bergamot oil, light it and say nine times:

> Fears and woes – I take respite
> Worries and cares – get out of sight
> Stronger and happier, I grow each day
> Now my soul has found its way

Charm for losing weight

The moon waxing and waning can be used to help you lose weight, although you should consider carefully why you want to lose weight and who you are doing it for. This spell will only work if you are doing it for yourself and if you are doing it in a healthy and responsible way. On a disc of wood or paper draw a full moon flanked by two crescent moons. On the first night of a waxing moon stand out in the garden bathed in the light of the moon and say:

> As you wane, so will I

Keep the disc on you at all times and if you feel your new healthy regime is slipping, hold the disc and reaffirm your reasons for wanting to lose weight.

A wishing tree

Write on a ribbon a wish for the world, a wish for friends and family and finally one for yourself. Tie the ribbon onto a special tree where the gentle breeze will spread your well-wishes. You can ask any visitor to your home to do the same. This is especially good to do around Yule time where they can be put on the traditional tree instead of baubles.

4

Sites

Somerset

Glastonbury

The magical town of Glastonbury can be found just off junction 23 of the M5 at the junction of the A39 and A361.

This magical town was once home to ancient Celts who called the place *Ynys-witrin* or The Isle of Glass and considering it was once marsh land surrounded by water, it's not surprising. After the Christian conversion it became home to a large Benedictine Abbey and up until about forty years ago was very much just a place of Christian pilgrimage. The abbey ruins remain as a testament to this time and so do the myths connected with it. It is now believed that back in medieval times the monks perpetrated a myth that the Biblical figure Joseph of Arimathea came to Glastonbury where upon, they said, he planted his staff into the ground and a hawthorn tree miraculously rose up. This tree is supposed to have 'magical' powers and is believed to be immortal, flowering unusually at Christmas time, imbuing it with deep relevance. Grafts of the original tree can be found in many places in Glastonbury, the two main ones being in the abbey grounds and on Weary-All Hill. He is also supposed to have bought the 'Holy Grail' or chalice from the last supper to Glastonbury which he buried there, there is a cup that was excavated and it is kept at Chalice Well Gardens; some still believe to this day that it is the real thing. But the monks were only trying to put their monastery on the map, none of their

Figure 11. Glastonbury Tor.

claims can be verified and most modern clergy today dispute its authenticity.

Since the resurgence of interest in the pagan and occult world, Glastonbury became of new interest to those pursuing anything from occult Western Mysteries to Witchcraft. People such as Dion Fortune and Wesley Tudor Pole were some of the early founders of magical groups that claimed Glastonbury as both a source of inspiration and a sanctuary for mystical enquirers.

Glastonbury has a lot to offer in a condensed space. You can take a wander up the infamous Tor, thought to be many things from the gateway to the fairy realm and the spiritual resting place of ancient Celts to King Arthur's burial mound, all of which is open to conjecture. There are two unusual springs that emanate from under the Tor. One is the Red spring, so called because it is rich in iron and leaves a red stain. The medieval monks profited from this anomaly also by saying it represented the blood of Christ. The red spring water can be obtained from Chalice Well Gardens, a highly magical place sympathetically managed, in which even the most ardent sceptic can have a truly spiritual experience. Then there is the white spring which is chalky and emerges from the other side of the road behind the gardens.

It would be hard not to notice the strong Witchcraft essence of the town with so many esoteric shops, healers, divinators and witches proliferating in this once exclusively Christian abbey town. The Christian element is still very much in evidence and it is good to see that these once completely opposed groups now reside reasonably peacefully alongside one another.

Stanton Drew

Just south of Bristol, off the A37 on the first turning on the right (the B3130), you come to Stanton Drew. Here you can see the Devils Wedding, a group of ancient standing stones. It's said that a wedding took place here long ago and the musician grew tired of playing and refused to continue after midnight on account of it being a Sunday. The bride wished to continue, however, and even said she'd go to hell to get a piper where upon an old man appeared and offered to play for them, the musician played faster and faster, with none of the party able to stop themselves from dancing. By morning, the villagers found nothing but the stones, which remain there to this day. There is also another myth attached to these stones, it is considered unlucky to attempt to count them or else risk becoming one yourself.

Stogumber

This typical Somerset village can be found by taking the A358 from Taunton, turning left onto the B3224. You will pass signs to Coombe Sydenham House, the place linked with Sir Francis Drake and his marriage to Elizabeth Sydenham. It is here that the alleged magically manifested canon ball is housed.

Taunton

This large Somerset town can be found off the M5, at junction 25. It has plenty of history to explore and is linked to several witch trials and one execution that we have already mentioned earlier in the book. Famous now for its cider making, Taunton makes a good base for exploring the western parts of Somerset and is also handy for Exmoor and the Quantock hills.

Wincanton

The town of Wincanton can be reached on the A303 main tourist road to the West Country, because of this it is often a very busy road and can become congested in peak season. Famous for its race course, it has made history here by being home to one of the Somerset covens not convicted of Witchcraft. Blackmoor Vale and Abbas Coombe nearby are where you are most likely to find modern witches practicing today.

Wookey Hole Caves

Just north of Wells, a city well worth visiting, you can find the Wookey Hole caves, which can be approached from either the A39 or the A371 and are well sign posted.

Here in the dark damp depths you are transported back in time to a place that feels very pre-historic. The river Axe flows through the caves and evidence of its occupation during the Stone Age has been excavated in the past. One of the stalagmites is meant to be the 'Witch of Wookey'. It's said that a witch once lived in the caves with her familiars, a goat and its kid, and that she was scorned by a lover which turned her sour and caused her to ill wish and cast spells against the local villagers. They in turn asked a local monk to visit the witch and deal with her evil ways. He threw Holy water on her, where upon she was turned to stone. Remains of a Romano British woman were found in the caves with various accoutrements including a comb, a dagger and a round object not unlike a crystal ball. The bones of a goat and kid were also discovered. All of these are now housed at Wells museum.

Devon

Belstone

Belstone can be reached off the A30 Okehampton By-Pass by taking the fourth turning on the left after the junction of the A3124. It lies at the edge of Dartmoor near the National Trust's Finch Foundry. Many of the pretty villages around this area make good bases for exploring this part of the moor with Cawsand Beacon the highest point nearby, standing at 548 feet above sea level and easily visible from quite a distance.

The area to the south is probably some of the wildest and most dramatic parts of Dartmoor and will give you a real flavour of ancient Britain and its magical energy. But don't underestimate this place, there is a very good reason for our own military utilising the moor as training ground for survival training. Although it can be beautiful and enticing in summer the further into the moor you go the wilder and less predictable the weather can become. It's often said that Dartmoor has its own weather system and with fog and mists appearing out of nowhere, it is quite a geographical challenge. The moor is surprisingly rocky and the hills can be steeper than they look so go prepared!

Bideford

To find the old town of Bideford you just head west on the north Devon part of the A39. It is a great position for touring this part of the north Devon coast with Westward Ho! and its sandy beaches just up the road. Bideford lies on the river Torridge with the larger town of Barnstaple just further north. To the south there is the town of Torrington, a mini Mecca for artists and other creative types, somewhere you are definitely likely to find modern day pagans and witches.

Dartmoor

The moor covers such a large area it is impossible to define a singular approach to the place. The northern most area can be reached from Okehampton, on the A30. The eastern most part is accessible off the A38, on the B3344 at Bovey Tracey. The southern area can be reached from the A38 at Ivybridge, and the western part from the A386 at Tavistock.

This mystical landscape is not what it first appears to be, one could easily mistake it for a natural example of untamed Britain but this is not so. The Neolithic, bronze, iron and medieval ages have all left their mark on Dartmoor. In fact one could go so far as to say they created it. This was once a heavily forested area with deer, boar and other wildlife living here in relative peace until the arrival of farming. Gradually the forests were cleared and crops were grown but our ancestors were not much better at sustainability than us and eventually the soil became impoverished and unsuitable for growing and so they left to find more fertile

Figure 12. Spinsters Rock on Dartmoor near Castle Drogo.

ground. The resulting peat bogs and standing stones, barrows and quoits that now inhabit the stark but dramatic landscape of Dartmoor are their legacy. This has left a ghostly haunted feel to the moor as if the ancestors and their spirits still walk the place and it is this that most practitioners of Witchcraft in the area most probably pick up on.

Much of the moor comes under the Duchy of Cornwall as do many parts of the West Country and it is the Duchy and current Prince of Wales we have to thank for maintaining much of the land as open and accessible to all.

Interesting places include:

Ceremonial sites at; Shovel Down (map ref 660859) with parking nearby (map ref 662866), Merrivale (map ref 555748) with parking close by.

And settlements at Grimspound (map ref 701809) with parking (map ref 697809), not too far to walk highly recommended. Foales Arishes settlement (map ref 738759) with parking at (map ref 7427610) close by.

More information can be found in Ancient Dartmoor an Introduction by Paul White of Bossiney Books ISBN 1-899383-22-0

South Molton

Found on the A361 Tiverton to Barnstaple road.

The ancient medieval market town of South Molton was once a thriving place for farmers from all over central Devon to converge on each week to sell their livestock and other wares. Although the market still exists it's a far cry from its hay-day but the town is in a good position for exploring some of the less well known parts of Devon and its beautiful rolling hills. This area is rich in history and no stranger to witches past and present drawing many who just want to escape the modern rat-race and take life at a slower pace. With its surrounding pretty little thatched villages it can easily take you back in time to the days of the cunning man and wise women. We are sure you could find yourself rubbing up against modern pagans and witches in the local bars but might not even know it, unless you ask.

Cornwall

Bodmin

The ancient town of Bodmin can be reached by travelling along the A30, across Bodmin Moor. The moor has long associations with paganism and witchcraft with some lovely examples of ancient stone circles such as The Hurlers near Upton Cross on the B3254, Trethevy Quoit just south near Tremar and the Anglo- Saxon village Merry Meet, further south, just off the A390, near Liskeard.

The highest point on the moor is the rather amusingly named Brown Willy, with the summit easily reached by reasonably fit people, standing at 419 feet above sea level.

This moor has a wild untamed feel about it and is quite small in comparison to Dartmoor but it still has its myths, not least of all the one relating to the occasional sightings of Jan Tregeagle's ghost running terrified from the 'whist hounds'. This 1660 magistrate lead an unholy life by all accounts and was accused of being in league with the devil. He returned from the grave after death and materialised in the assizes in Bodmin in one case, his ghost was sent to the bottom of Witches Pool.

But even this didn't hold him and, to cut a very long story short, he kept appearing in differing districts whenever anyone called his name. The clergy of each district sent his spirit to the next until, it's said, he ended up at Lands End.

The more recent sightings of 'the beast of Bodmin' are debatable but, in essence, there are many who claim to have seen a large black cat roaming the moor. The reputably haunted Jamacia Inn can be easily accessed from the A30 and is situated about half way across the moor. Traffic late morning and early afternoon in high season can be very heavy though.

Boscastle

Off the A39 North Atlantic Highway on the B3263.

This pretty little Cornish village made national headline news on the 16th August, 2004, as the whole village suffered a dreadful flood nearly destroying every building in its path, indeed it was a miracle no one was actually killed. The village is home to The Museum of Witchcraft run by owner and curator Graham King. As Graham is also a coast guard he instantly found himself the only qualified and trained person in the village having to deal and react quickly to what was fast becoming a major incident. It is partly due to his quick thinking and early alert that everyone involved survived with only a few injuries sustained. But this wasn't magic or witchcraft just plain efficient and brave handling of a potentially catastrophic situation for the village as a whole.

Although the museum suffered much flood damage, the building is still intact and the vast majority of the artefacts were salvaged. Since the incident, Graham has received much support from the Pagan community with some donated objects, funds and new books for the library being offered and even some lovely display cases sent by the Natural History museum. The National Maritime Museum offered dry storage space for some of the flood damaged books for a while which they were very grateful for.

The original owner, Cecil Williamson, sold the museum to Graham at midnight on 31st October, 1996. Cecil has since passed away but many of his papers and artefacts remain.

Graham also maintains an extensive esoteric library which can be accessed with acceptable references by arrangement.

I visited Boscastle nearly a year on and was incredibly impressed with how far the restoration work had advanced, the work is nearly completed with only a few buildings left to re-build and one of the bridges, it has been carried out with real sympathy for the authenticity of the original look and feel of the village. This was an emotional pilgrimage for me as Boscastle was the first ever place in Cornwall I visited back in 1983, and it initiated me into a life long love affair with the north Cornish coast. Nestling deep in a little valley, the dramatic cliffs beyond the harbour and the rugged exposed coastline is like stepping back in time to the days of smugglers, pirates and simple fishermen. It offers a real sense of close West Country community life. The museum is very much alive and well and is well worth visiting if you get the chance.

Helston on the A394

According to folk lore the Devil was flying across Cornwall carrying a boulder to use to block the entrance to Hell when he was met by St. Michael. A battle ensued, the Devil dropped the rock and the place where it fell became known as 'Hells Stone' or Helston. That boulder is said to be found today in the wall of The Angel Hotel in Coinagehall Street.

To celebrate the victory over the Devil the inhabitants danced through the streets in what is called the Furry dance or, latterly, the Floral Dance.

This still takes place on the nearest Saturday to the feast day of the town's patron saint, St. Michael the Archangel (8th May). The dance gets underway at midday to the beat of a bass drum. The dance is always lead by a couple who were born in Helston. The name of the dance is thought to have come from the English word 'Ferrie' which means a church festival or, and this is what we think more likely, from the Celtic word 'feur' meaning a holiday or fair.

This occurring in May suggests that the dance may also have been a pagan spring celebration to make sure that the land was fertile for a good harvest. The town is festooned with bluebells and hazel. The dance steps have never changed, the gentlemen all wear shirt and ties and the ladies wear light summer dresses with lily of the valley in their hair.

The Hal-an-Tow is a mumming play that is re-enacted by the older children of the town and it precedes the Furry

Dance, garlanded and carrying branches of sycamore they sing:

> Welcome is the summer, the summer and the May-O
> For summer is a-come-O and winter is a-gone-O?

They also sing about St. George and the dragon, Robin Hood and the Spanish Armada.

Mên-an-Tol 2½ miles west of Madron on the B3306

This circle and stone complex is thought to aid divination and has curative powers. The name simply means 'holed stone' and refers to the central stone in the present arrangement of three stones in a row. The holed stone is supposed to cure ailments and will also perform ocular functions. The stone was particularly renowned for its curative properties in respect of children suffering from rickets and also 'scrofulus taint' which is tuberculosis of the lymph glands of the neck. The curative ritual for children consists of passing them naked through the stone three times and then drawing them three times widdershins round it. The word widdershins is Saxon in origin and means literally 'wider/vider shin' against the sun, so anti-clockwise. Adults with spinal diseases or scrofula were said to have been successfully treated by being drawn through this magic stone.

The Mên-an-Tol was also used for augury, it was said that if two brass pins were carefully laid across each other on the top edge, any question put to them would be answered by the various movements of the pins. Age-old myths think this is due to spirits in the stones and guardian spirits that dwell in sacred places. Holed stoneswere used for sealing marriage vows; couples would plight their troth holding hands through the hole in the stone. They were also used to seal contracts, grasping hands through the hole.

Lostwithiel

This can be found on the A390 just south of Bodmin on the river Fowey. Like many places in Cornwall it has been a haven for

Witches and magical practitioners over the centuries. The modern day Charmer Ivan Miller can be found here but we don't have an actual contact number or address so if looking him up it's probably best just to ask around the pubs or local gathering places. It is a better alternative than St. Austell for a quiet spot to explore the area from and places that we can recommend are The Eden Project and the Lost Gardens of Heligan both of which are nearby. It is also handy for the southern part of Bodmin Moor.

Merry Maidens (Rosemodress) B3315

This astounding circle can be found situated in a small field to the south west of the Lamorna valley on the road that leads from Newlyn to Lands End. It is a near perfect circle with all the stones standing after being restored in the 1860s. Another popular name for this circle is 'Dans Mean' *i.e.* stone dance, due to them being in a circular order making an area for dancing.

The local folklore tells of the ring representing nine maidens who were turned to stone for dancing on a Sunday. There are two upright stones standing near this circle and these are known as the pipers those that provided the music for the maidens to dance to, who were also petrified for merrymaking on the Sabbath.

Other old tales say that the Merry Maidens was a place of great military conflict. In one story it was the site of a battle between Saxons and Celts in 936 AD. In this legend it is the place from which the two kings (Howell for Cornwall and Athelstan for Saxony) directed their troops. Alternatively it is said that King Arthur fought there against the Saxons.

The Merry Maidens, along with other circles in the area represent the remains of what must once have been important ceremonial sites. The few burial mounds that still remain are likely to be vestiges of large barrows that were the resting place for the dead. This fits in well with the dancing and merrymaking as the ceremonies for the living and the dead were inextricably entwined as part of the great circle of life.

Newlyn A30, B3315

Although this has place no connection to witchcraft, my lasting memory of my childhood trips to Newlyn is the famous Cornish Clotted Cream ice cream from a tiny family run shop in the middle of the village, well worth a trip out for.

This is a beautiful village with a long history of fishing, there is a spectacular art gallery and a fishing museum to visit. But be wary of any little old ladies carrying cowls of fish, be sure to get out of her way as it could be an ancestor of Dolly Pentreath and you don't want to be cursed by her!!

Padstow

This very old fishing village can be located off the A39 Atlantic highway on the A389, just on the edge of the Camel estuary. Padstow was originally named Petroc-stow after St. Petroc, whose claim to fame was his striking of a rock that magically produced a stream of water. Padstow is home to the annual 'Obby Oss' May Day celebrations. The origins of this custom are not entirely clear, some saying it relates directly to ancient pagan fertility traditions. Others say it re-enacts the legend of St. George slaying the Dragon, either way it is a most fascinating spectacle. There are actually two 'oss's' involved, both of which do circuits of the town throughout the day collecting money for local good causes. The event attracts people from all over by the thousand and has in some respects out grown the town but it is still well worth seeing and being a part of if you get the chance.

The Witches of Padstow, past and present, are here but not so obviously and one has to be fairly tactful in ones enquiries. Like most of the fishing villages on the Cornish coast, it has long associations with folklore, superstitions and witchcraft but today it is more famous for Rick Stein's Seafood restaurant and has since been amusingly referred to as 'Padstein' by locals.

St. Michaels Mount A394 at Marazion

Known locally as '*carrick luz en cuz*' or the 'ancient rock in the wood'. This is a familiar and stunning site in Cornwall, rising up out of the sea and at low tide the causeway that leads to it from the main land appearing like some secret path. Also, at low tide, the fossilised remains of a forest can be seen which would have surrounded St. Michaels Mount. On the mount there is a rough hewn stone seat which is called St. Michaels Chair. Apparently, St. Keyne was on a pilgrimage and decided to endow the chair with a particular property, if either a bride or a groom is the first to sit on the chair then they will have the upper hand in the marriage.

This is a spectacular place to visit but you do have to be wary of the tides as you can get stranded there if you are not careful, so check the times before you venture onto this magical rock.

Tintagel

The ancient town of Tintagel lies off the A39 Atlantic highway on the B3263. Tintagel has made a name for itself by claiming to be one of several possible sites for King Arthur's Castle but, although the town is definitely profiting from this potential attribute, it is highly unlikely to be historically accurate. Below the ruins two caves can be accessed at low tide, the one under the castle is thought to be Merlin's cave and it is said that if you obtain a stone from this cave it will bring you good luck, if you carelessly lose it however the opposite will occur.

The castle is very dramatic, occupying a high cliff top vantage point with most of it accessible by a stout wooden footbridge. English Heritage manages the site and offers an information point for interested parties to view. The site was built on by Reginald of Cornwall, Henry I's illegitimate son, long after the time of King Arthur and has also been used as a monastery.

Tintagel has attracted many modern day pagans and witches as a place of spiritual pilgrimage and there are several esoteric shops operating in the town.

Witches Stone

To find The Witches Stone, you need to travel south of Honiton to Putt's Corner on the large heath land there. One cannot miss The Witches Stone standing outside the local pub. The local superstition says that the stone rolls down the hill each night to wash itself in the river Syd to rid itself of the evil influence of witches. The area has a mystical feel to it being surrounded by woodland and might have been used by early Britons as a place of sacrifice but this misnomer is probably rooted in medieval paranoia.

Zennor B3306

In the local church there is a 15th Century bench which has the image of a mermaid carved into it. This refers to the local story of Matthew Trewella, a squire's son who was a chorister in that very church. He sang so beautifully that it attracted the attention of a mermaid, using all her charms she lured him back into her deep domain, from which he never returned. It is said that his voice can still be heard under the waves. Near by is a rock known as the Witches Rock. This has long been associated with local witches and Midsummer's Eve rituals, to touch the rock nine times at midnight is regarded as insurance against bad luck and can mean your instant initiation as a witch.

Magical West Country Shops

Aquarius Rising – Minehead
Arcania – Bath
Avalon – Falmouth
Crystal Chalice – Launceston
Emjems – St. Ives

Goddess and The Green Man – Glastonbury
Growing Needs – Glastonbury
King Arthur's Bookshop – Tintagel
Labyrinth – Glastonbury
Lavender Pillow – Mevagissey
Otherworld – Boscastle
Speaking Tree – Glastonbury
Starchild – Exeter

Bibliography

The Discoverie of Witchcraft by Reginald Scott publishers Dover Publications Inc. New York ISBN 0-486-26030-5

The Witch of the West by Jason Semmens self published available from the Witchcraft Museum, Boscastle

Occult in the West by Michael Williams published by Bossiney Books ISBN 0-906456-15-0

The Witchcraft and Folklore of Dartmoor by Ruth E. St. Leger-Gordon publishers Robert Hale London (out of print but occasionally pops up in second hand shops and on e-Bay)

The Psychology of Witchcraft by Tom Ravensdale & James Morgan publishers John Bartholomew and Son Ltd. (out of print, try second hand shops and e-Bay)

Devon's Witchcraft by A.Farquharson-Coe publishers James Pike Ltd. (can still be found occasionally on spinners)
White Witches, A Study of Charmers by Rose Mullins publishers PR Publishing ISBN 0-9533825-1-3

An Joan the Crone by Kelvin I. Jones publishers Oakmagic Publications ISBN 1-901163-93-8

A Witches Treasurary of the Countryside by Melusine Draco & Paul Harris publishers Ignotus Press ISBN 1-903768-08-X

Folklore Myths and Legends of Britain publishers Readers Digest (not sure if still in print)

West Country Wicca by Rhiannon Ryall publishers Capall Bann ISBN 1-898307-02-4

Ancient Dartmoor an Introduction by Paul White publishers Bossiney Books ISBN 1-899383-22-0

Thomas, Val, A Witch's Kitchen, Capall Bann, 2002

Beth, Rae, Hedge Witch, Hale, 1996

Worth, Valerie, Crone's Book of Charms & Spells, Llewellyn, 2002

Guiley, Rosemary Ellen, The Encyclopaedia of Witches and Witchcraft, Checkmark Books, 1999

Cope, Julian, The Modern Antiquarian, Thorsons, 1998